Classic Fine Art Nudes Volume Four

By

Carl Scott Harker

Copyright Notice

Cover design by Carl Scott Harker

Copyright © 2021 Carl Scott Harker

Note: The artworks presented in this book are in the public domain. The book, as published, is, of course, copyrighted.

An Aldouspi Publication

Table of Contents

Forward .... Page 5

Summer 1919 by Georges Barbier .... Page 7
Woman with Blue Blanket by Felix Vallotton .... Page 8
Beauty with Flowers Inside Hans Zatzka .... Page 9
Posed Models by Georges Seurat .... Page 10
Beauty Washing Hair by Shinsui Ito .... Page 11
Nude Woman by the River by Anders Zorn .... Page 12
Nymph of Spring 1550 by Lucas Cranach the Younger .... Page 13
The Boxer by Konstantin Somov .... Page 14
Witch on a Broomstick by Albert Joseph Pernot .... Page 15
Seated Nude by William H. Johnson .... Page 16
Water Nymph by Gaston Brussiere .... Page 17
Nude Bather 1918 by Edvard Munch .... Page 18
Nude on a Sofa by Leo Putz .... Page 19
Danae – Greek Princess by Jean Francois de Troy .... Page 20
Smoke By Louis Icart .... Page 21
Harem Beauties by Henri Adrien Tanoux .... Page 22
Nude on Blue Background by Ernst Kirchner .... Page 23
Nude Next to Radiator By Pierre Bonnard .... Page 24
Eh? You're Jealous? by Paul Gauguin .... Page 25
The Three Ages of Woman by Gustav Klimt .... Page 26
Nude Reclining on Sofa by Suzanne Valadon .... Page 27
Nude in the Clouds – Cover from La Vie Parisian 1925 .... Page 28
Two Nude Women by Water by Egon Schiele .... Page 29
Nude Male Leaning Against Box by Gustav Klimt .... Page 30
La Toilette by Frederic Bazille .... Page 31
Three Mermaids, 1879 by Hans Thoma .... Page 32
Morning in the City by Edward Hopper .... Page 33
Nude Woman in Bed by Toulouse Lautrec .... Page 34

Nude Standing by Vitaly Tikhov	Page 35
Bacchanale by Leo Putz	Page 36
Sarah Bernhardt by Georges Antoine Rochegrosse	Page 37
Orientalism - Nude Woman of the Harem by Gyula Tornai	Page 38
Nightclub Singer 1901 by Pablo Picasso	Page 39
Two Women by Felix Vallotton	Page 40
Portrait of Simonetta Vespucci 1480 by Piero di Cosimo	Page 41
Odalisque by Georges Rochegrosse	Page 42
Underwater Kingdom by Ilya Repin	Page 43
Antiope and Jupiter in the Form of a Satyr by Hendrick Goltzius	Page 44
Ancient Roman Slave by Oscar Pereira da Silva	Page 45
Nude Woman Miss Leslie Hall by George Bellows	Page 46
Bloodthirsty Erynnies Demon Vampires by Gustave Dore	Page 47
The Nude by Henri Lebasque	Page 48
In a Russian Banya by Vitaly Tikhov	Page 49
Nude Woman Unmasked by Akseli Gallen Kallela	Page 50
Nude on a Spring Morning by Henri Lebasque	Page 51
Girl with Blue Veil by Gustav Klimt	Page 52
Ancient Chinese Erotica – Nude Couple by Unknown	Page 53
Nude Woman with Black Cat by Alberto Vargas	Page 54
Lassitude - Nude Woman with Eyes Closed by Gari Melchers	Page 55
Nude 1914 by Murayama Kaita	Page 56
About the Author	Page 57
Other Books by the Author	Page 57

Forward

This fourth volume of classic fine art nudes continues in the tradition of being a mixture of different styles from different time periods celebrating the female form and the male form.

The nudes in this volume reflect a variety of purposes. Nudes are used to illustrate mythical stories such as the portrait of Danae – the mother of the Greek hero Perseus, or a mermaid leading a parade in an underwater kingdom. Or they may reflect a cultural fantasy such as harem women in the Orientalism movement of the 1880's and 1890's. Or they may be used as scintillating subjects of artists pursuing news ways to present art itself. The works of Leo Putz, Louis Icart and Henri Lebasque all present the nude form in unique ways, for example.

While each painting presented here represent the societies and times in which they were painted; they all transcend the parameters of the moment to be true works of art. The beauty and the fascination of the nude is explored in both classical and new ways.

As in past volumes, some of the artists in this book will be familiar to you and some may not be familiar you. Rest assured each work of art is worthy of your attention. Here are fifty great nudes – enjoy!

Summer 1919 by Georges Barbier

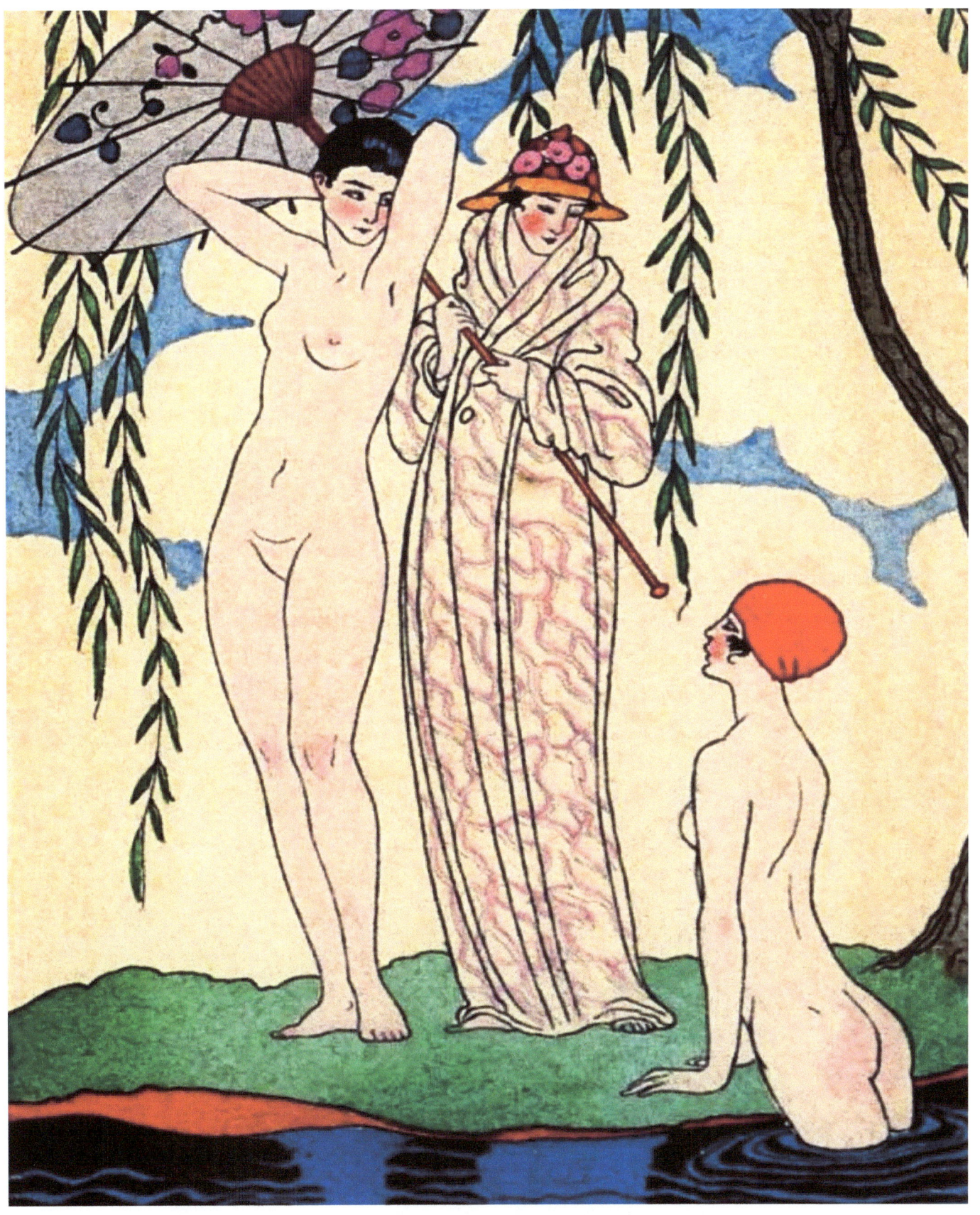

Woman with Blue Blanket by Felix Vallotton

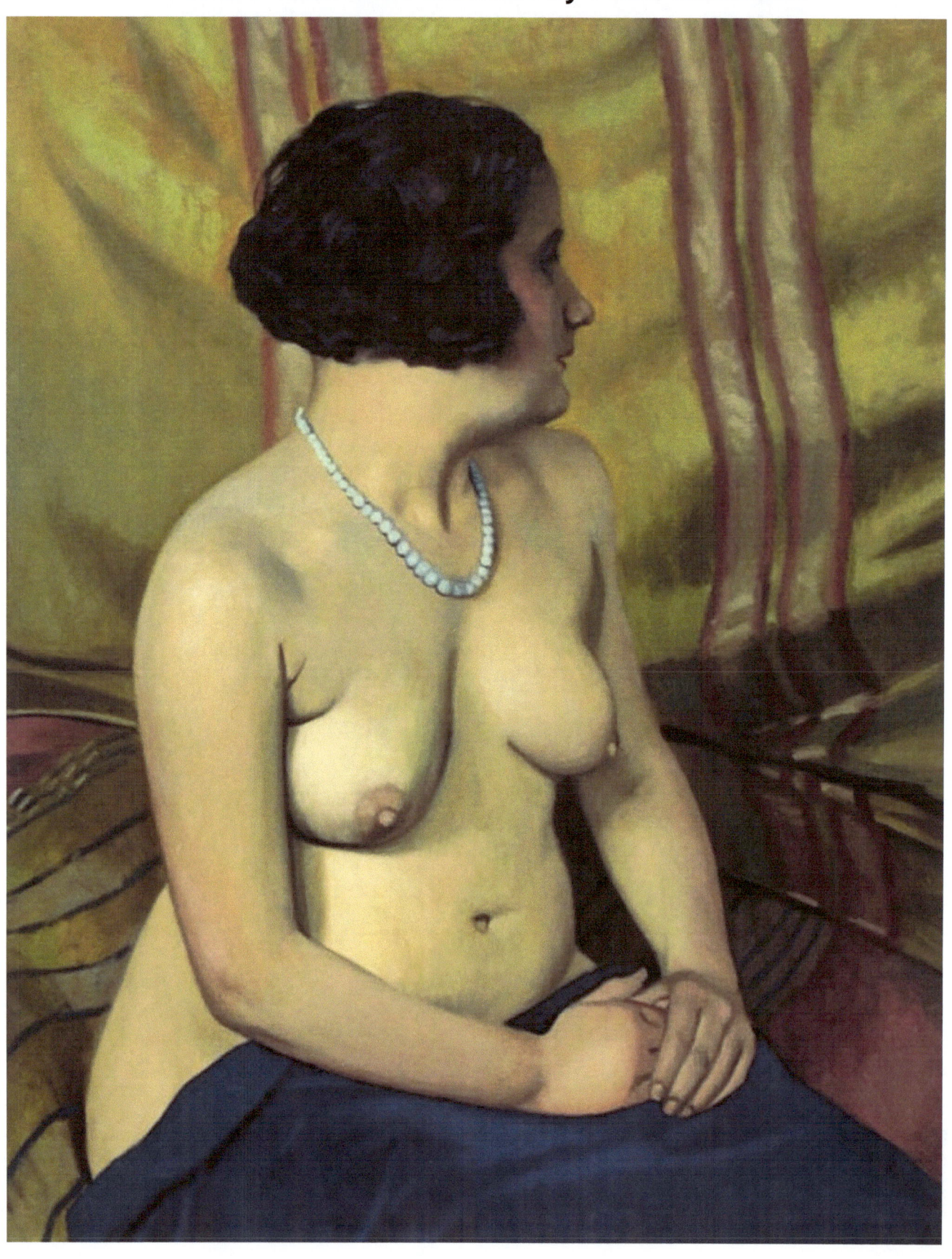

Beauty with Flowers Inside Hans Zatzka

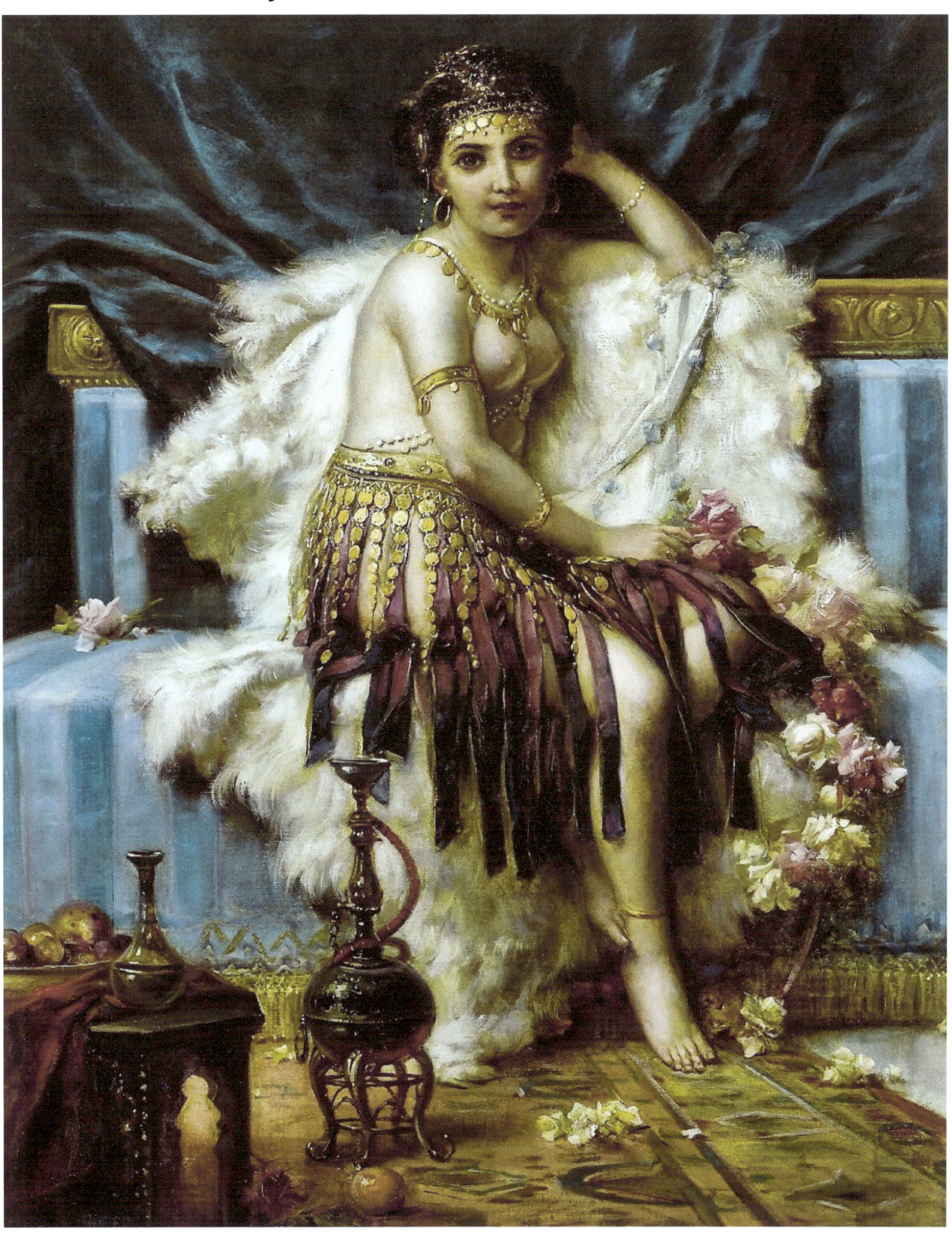

Posed Models by Georges Seurat

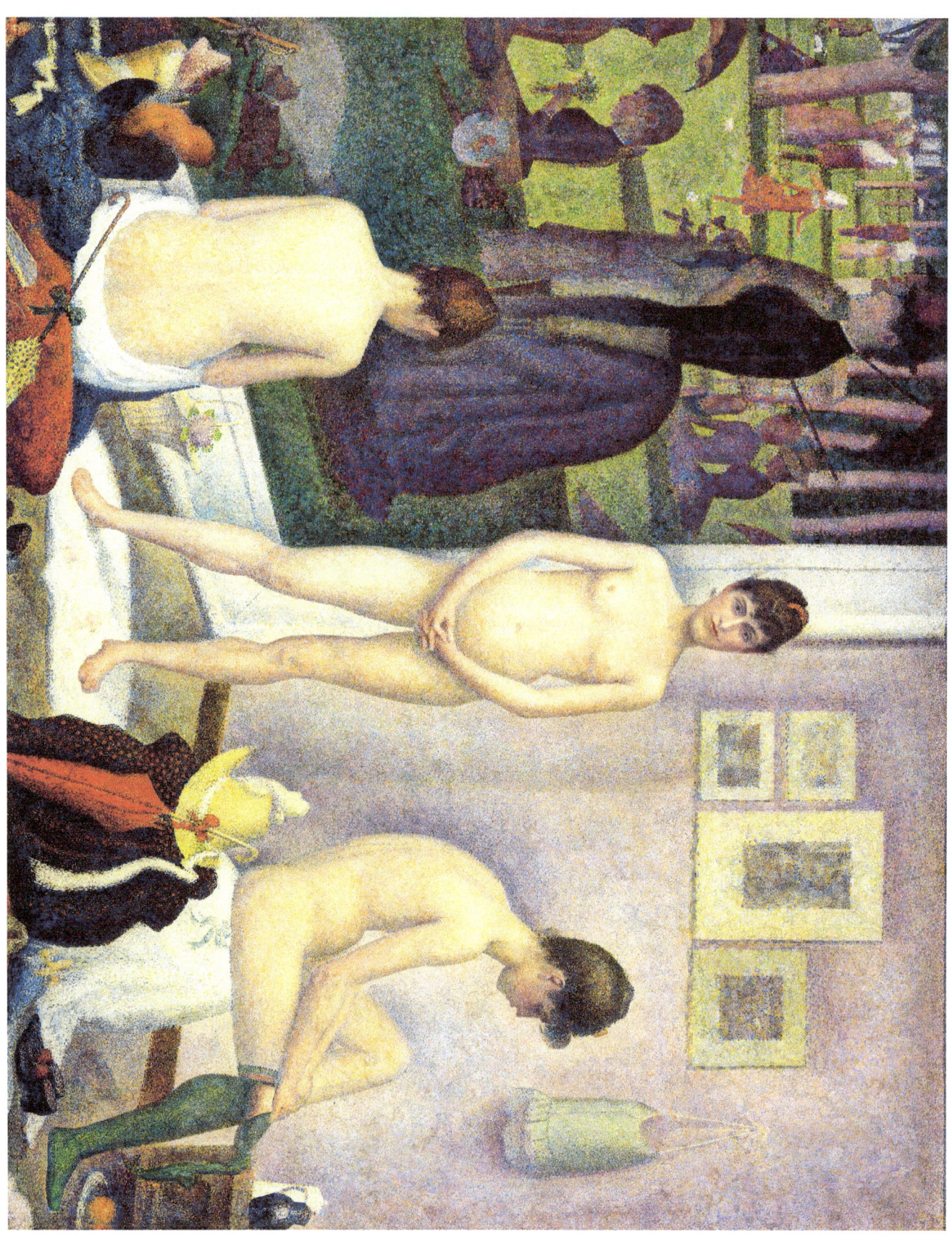

Beauty Washing Hair by Shinsui Ito

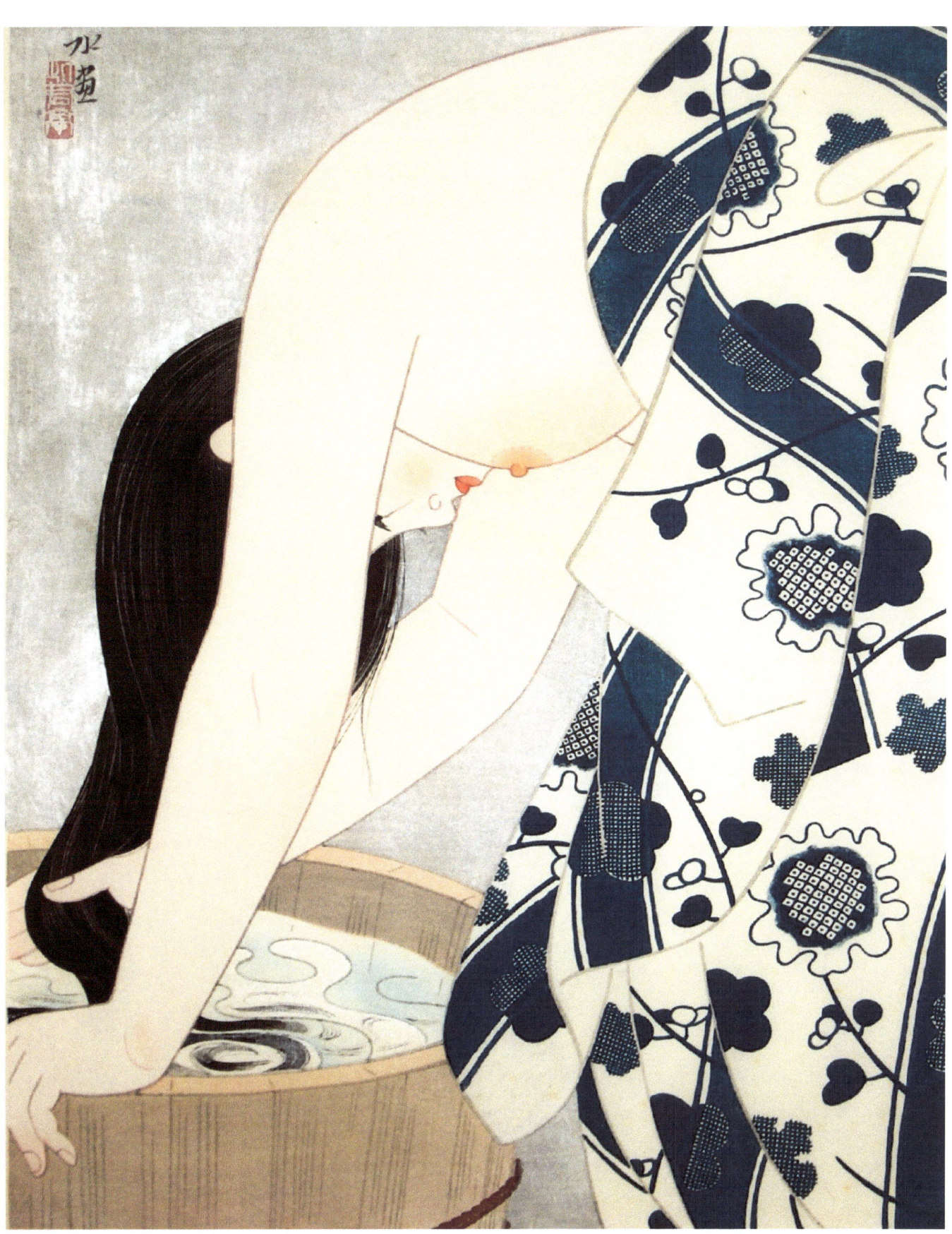

Nude Woman by the River by Anders Zorn

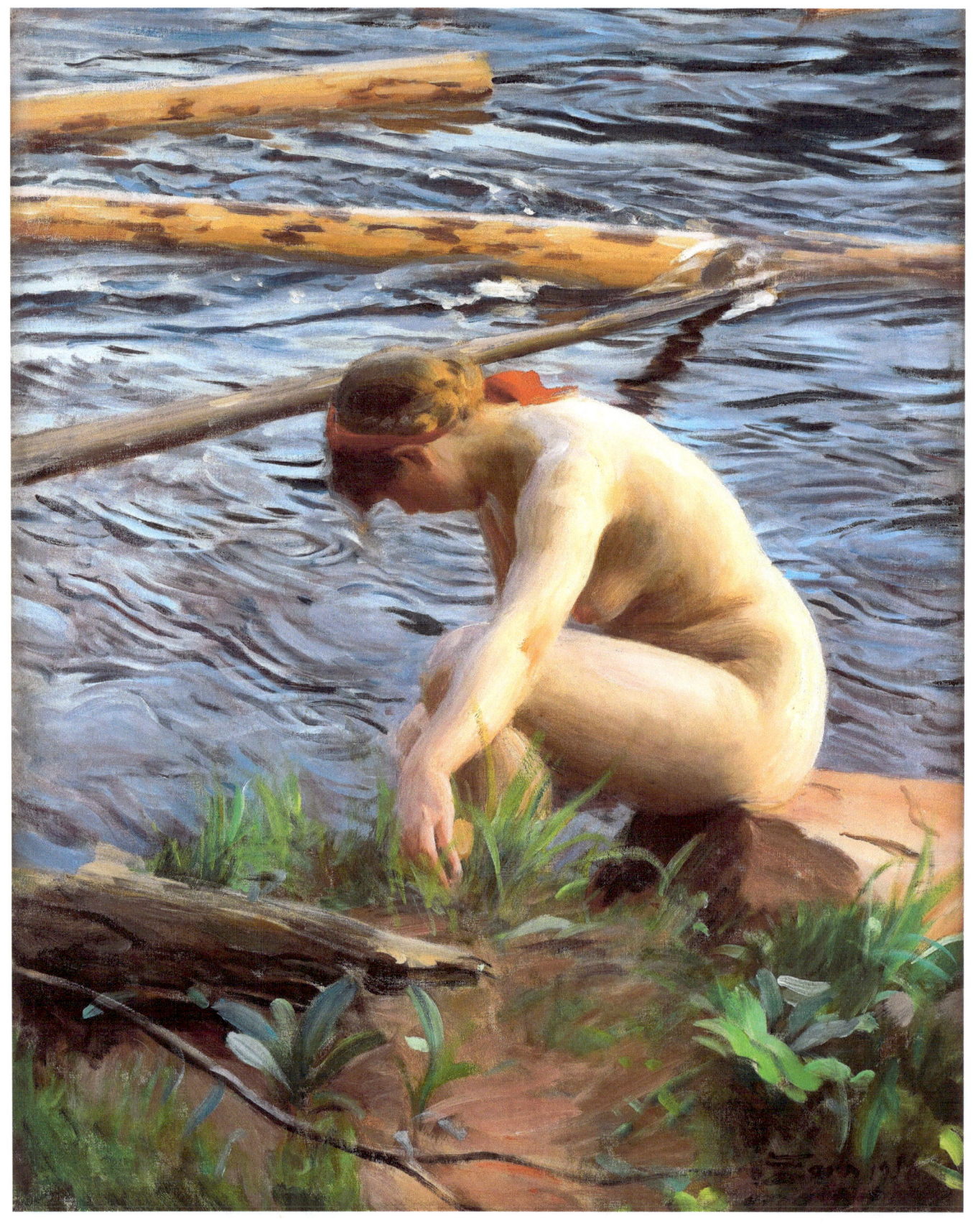

Nymph of Spring 1550 by Lucas Cranach the Younger

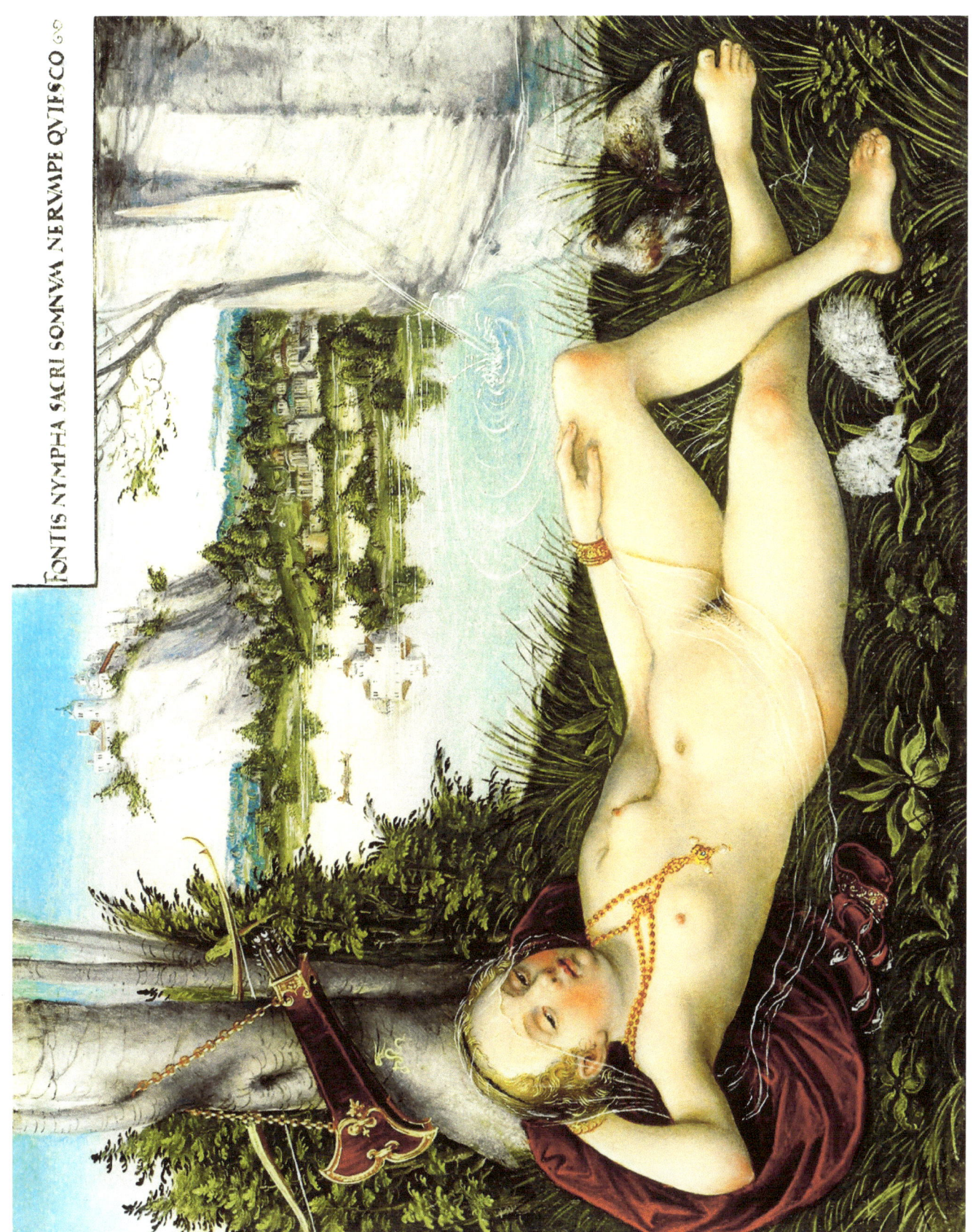

The Boxer by Konstantin Somov

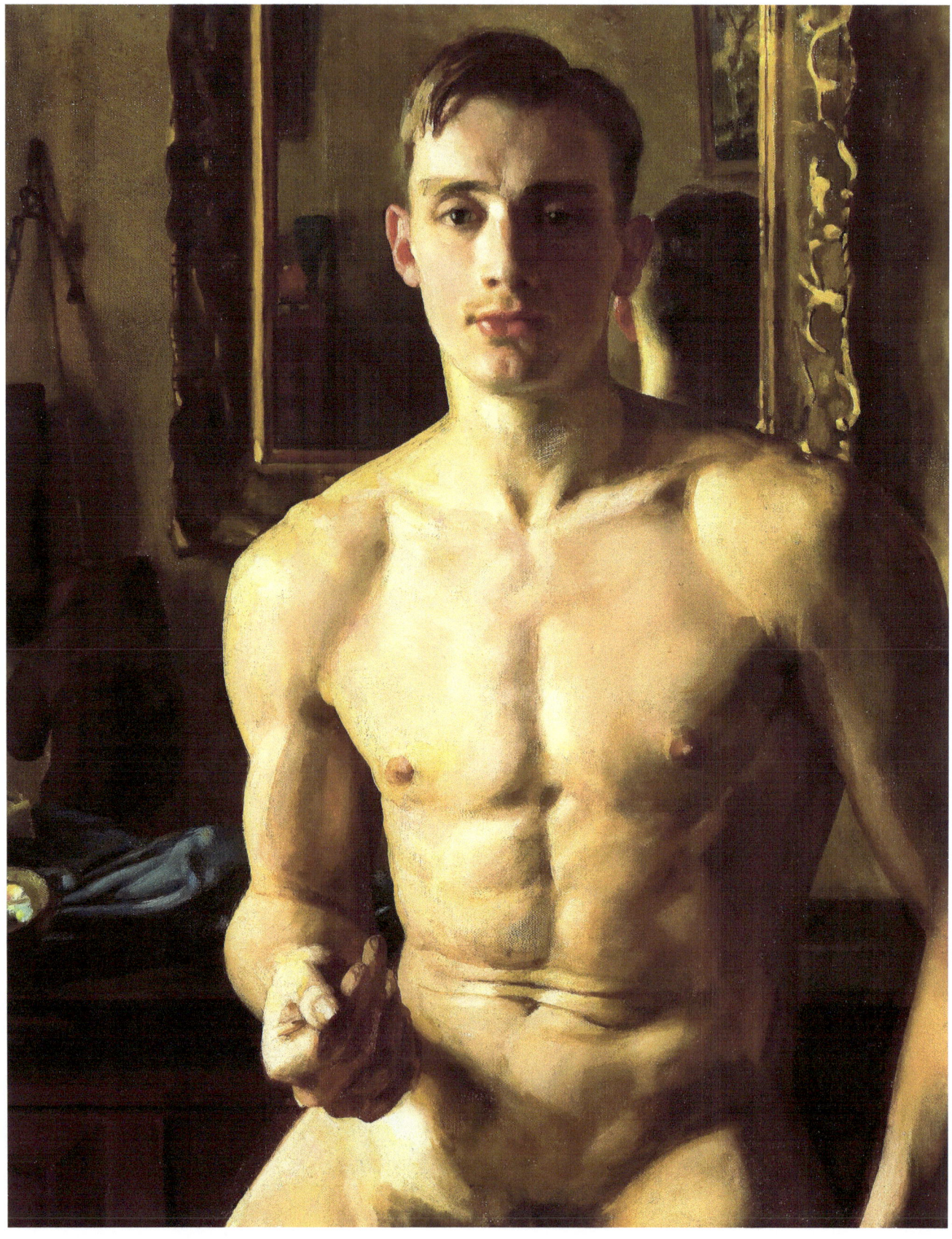

Witch on a Broomstick by Albert Joseph Pernot

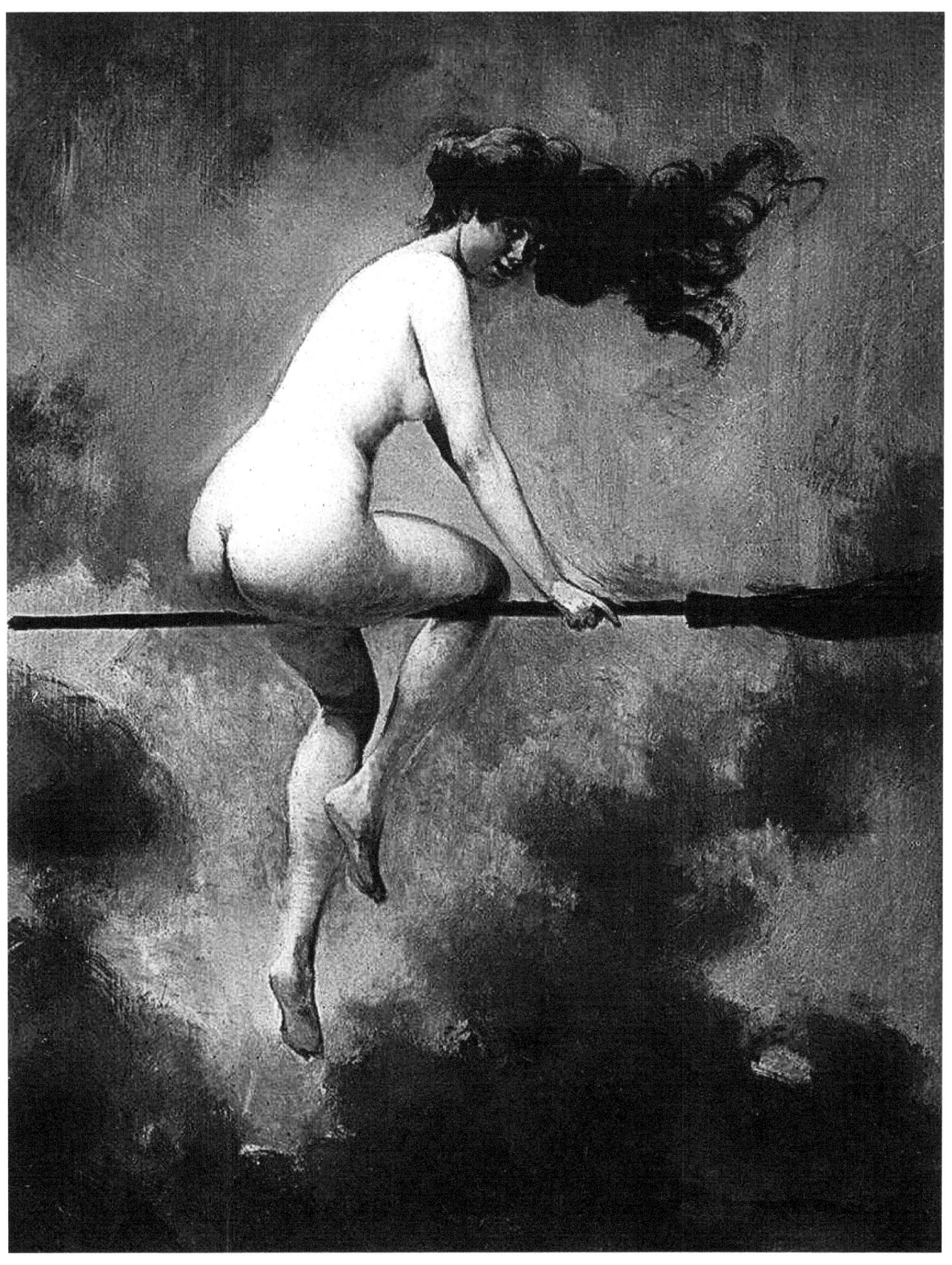

Seated Nude by William H. Johnson

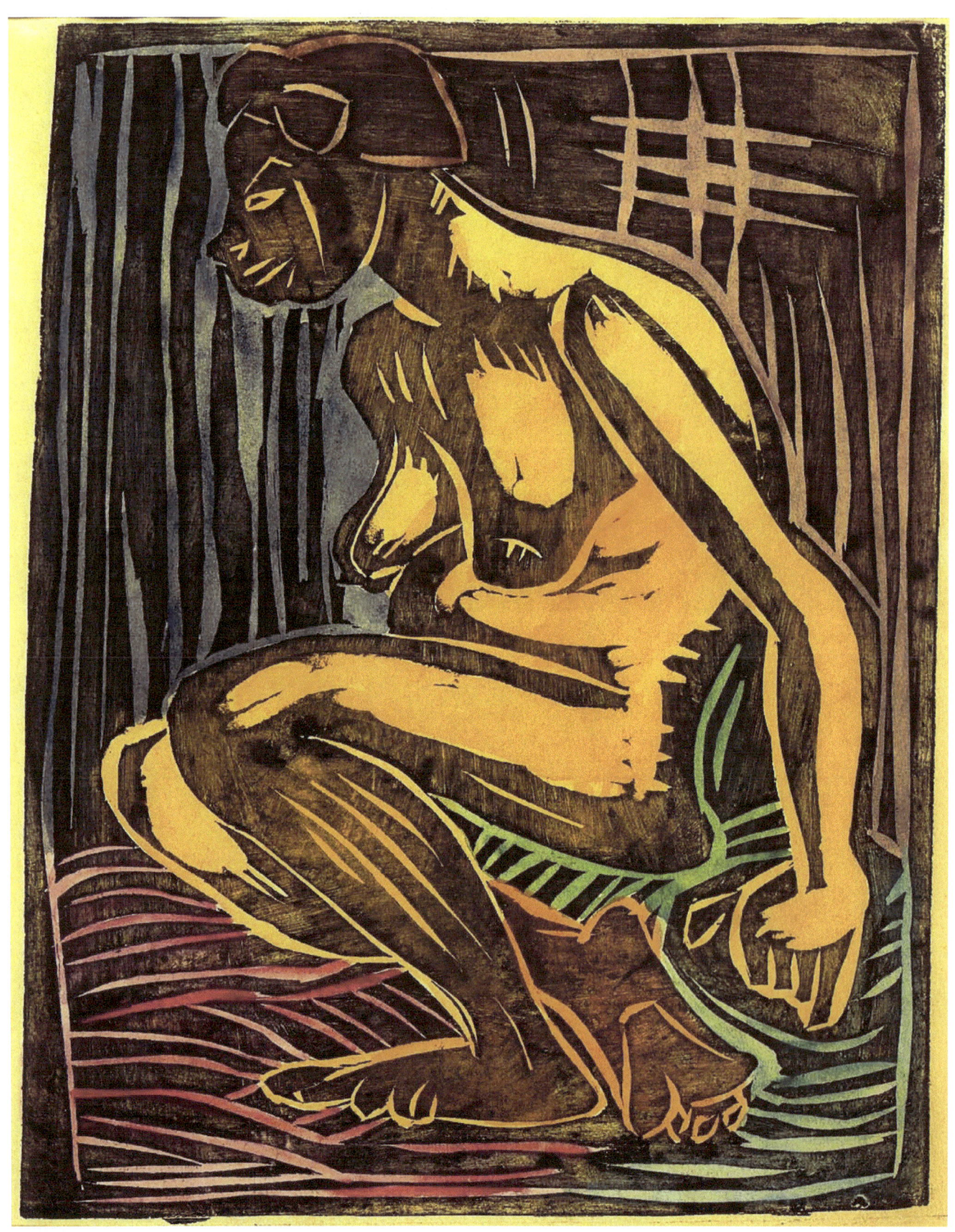

Water Nymph by Gaston Brussiere

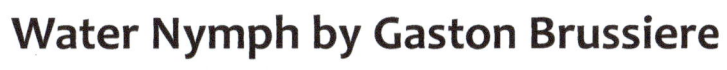

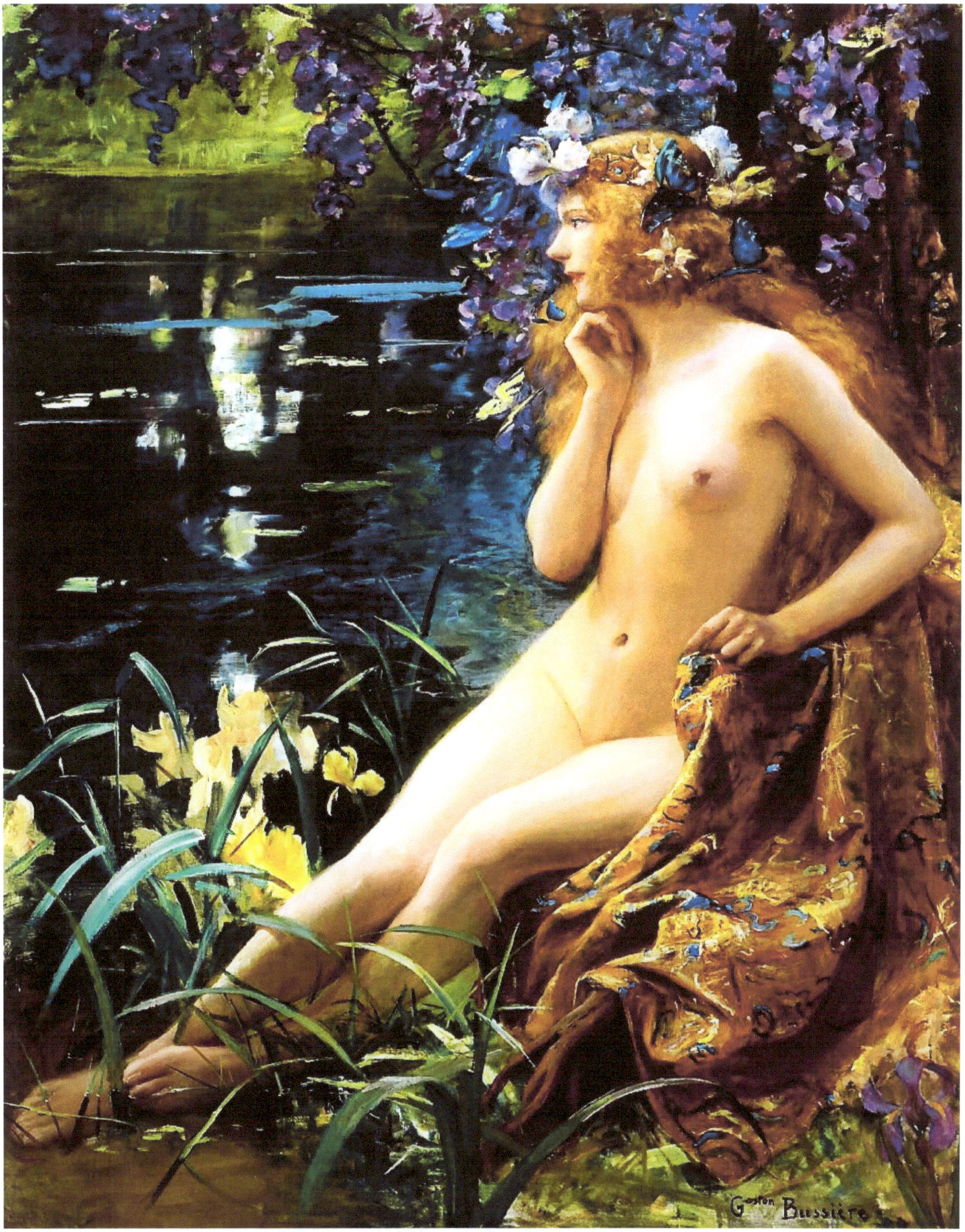

Nude Bather 1918 by Edvard Munch

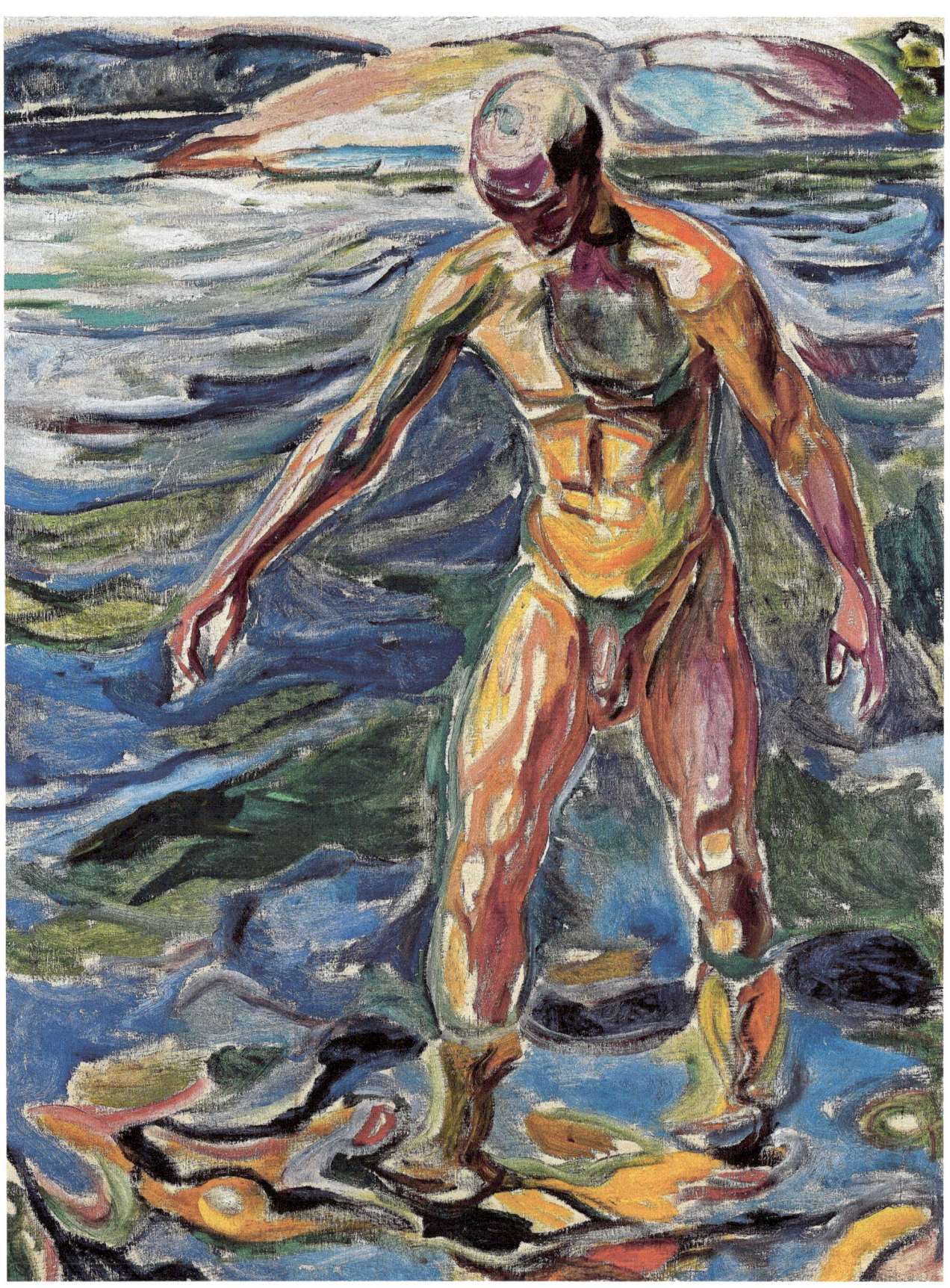

Nude on a Sofa by Leo Putz

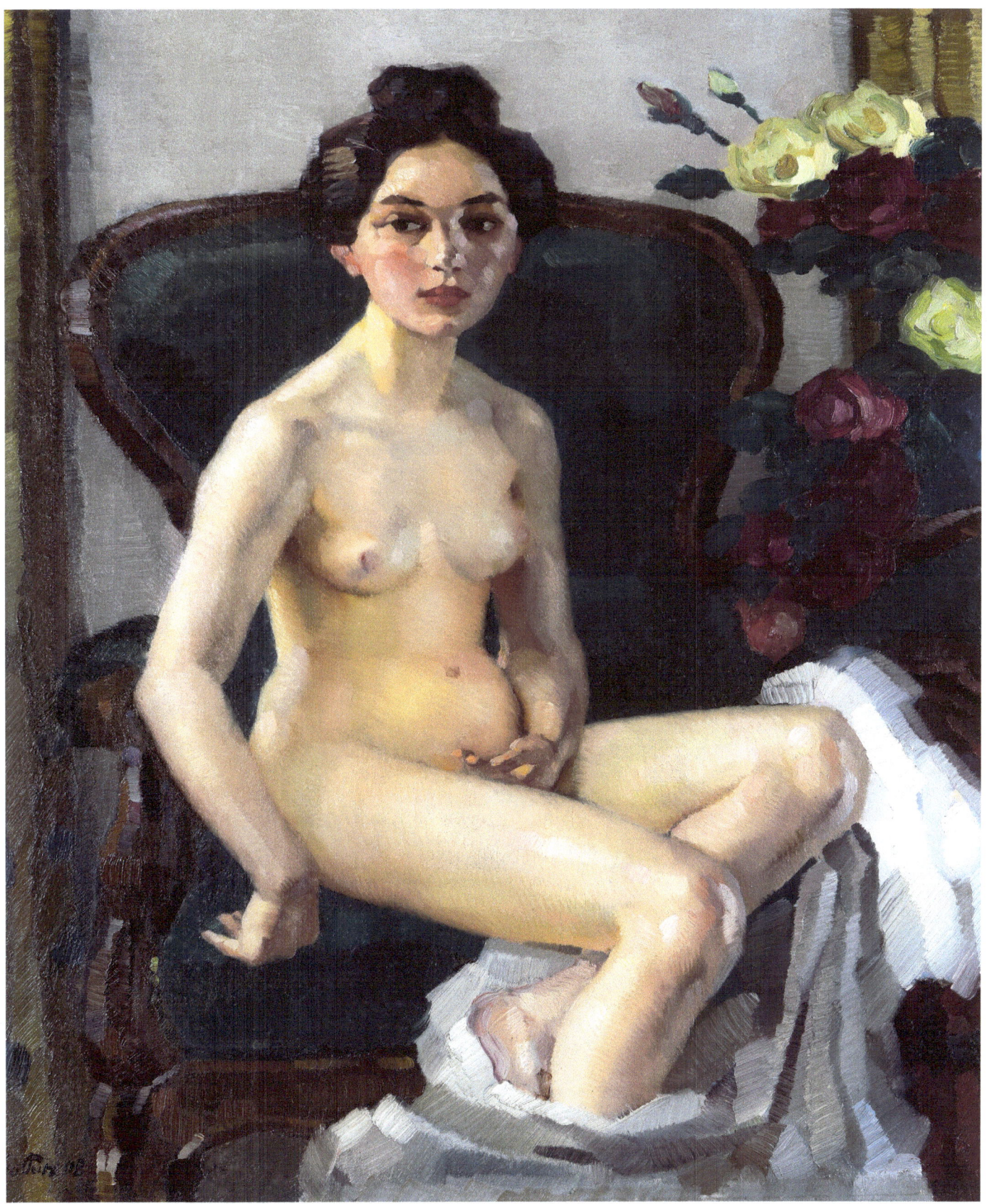

Danae – Greek Princess by Jean Francois de Troy

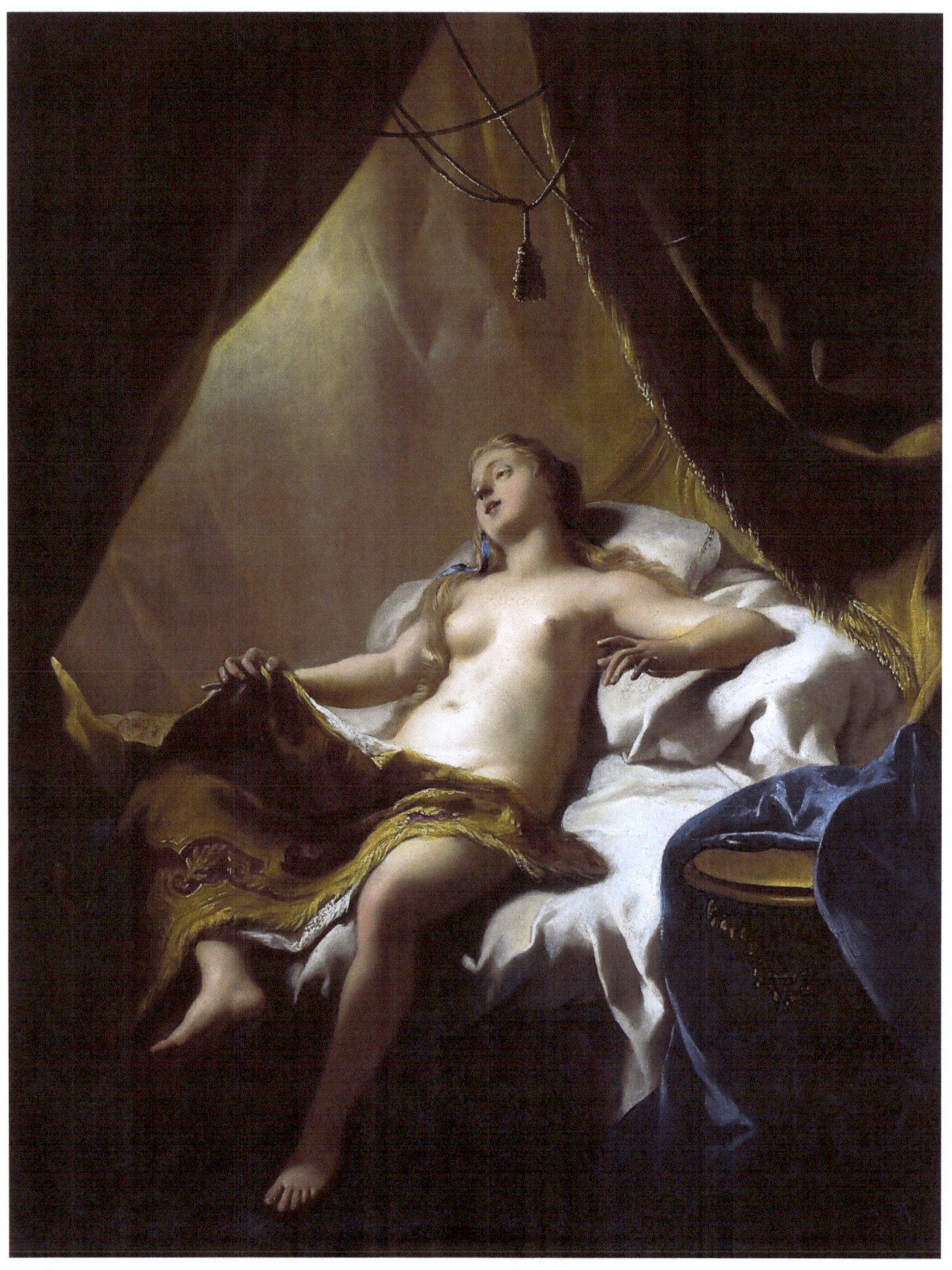

Smoke By Louis Icart

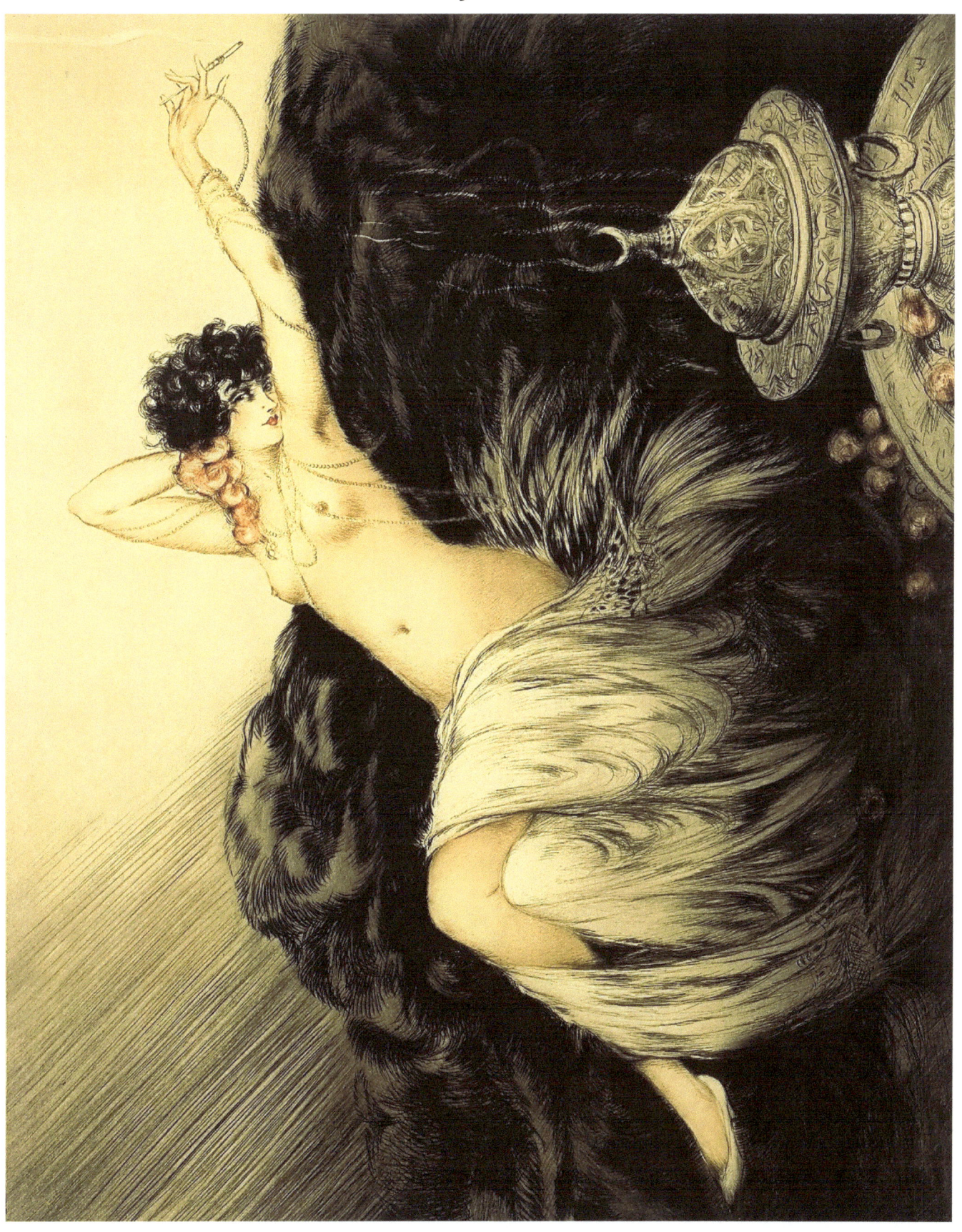

Harem Beauties by Henri Adrien Tanoux

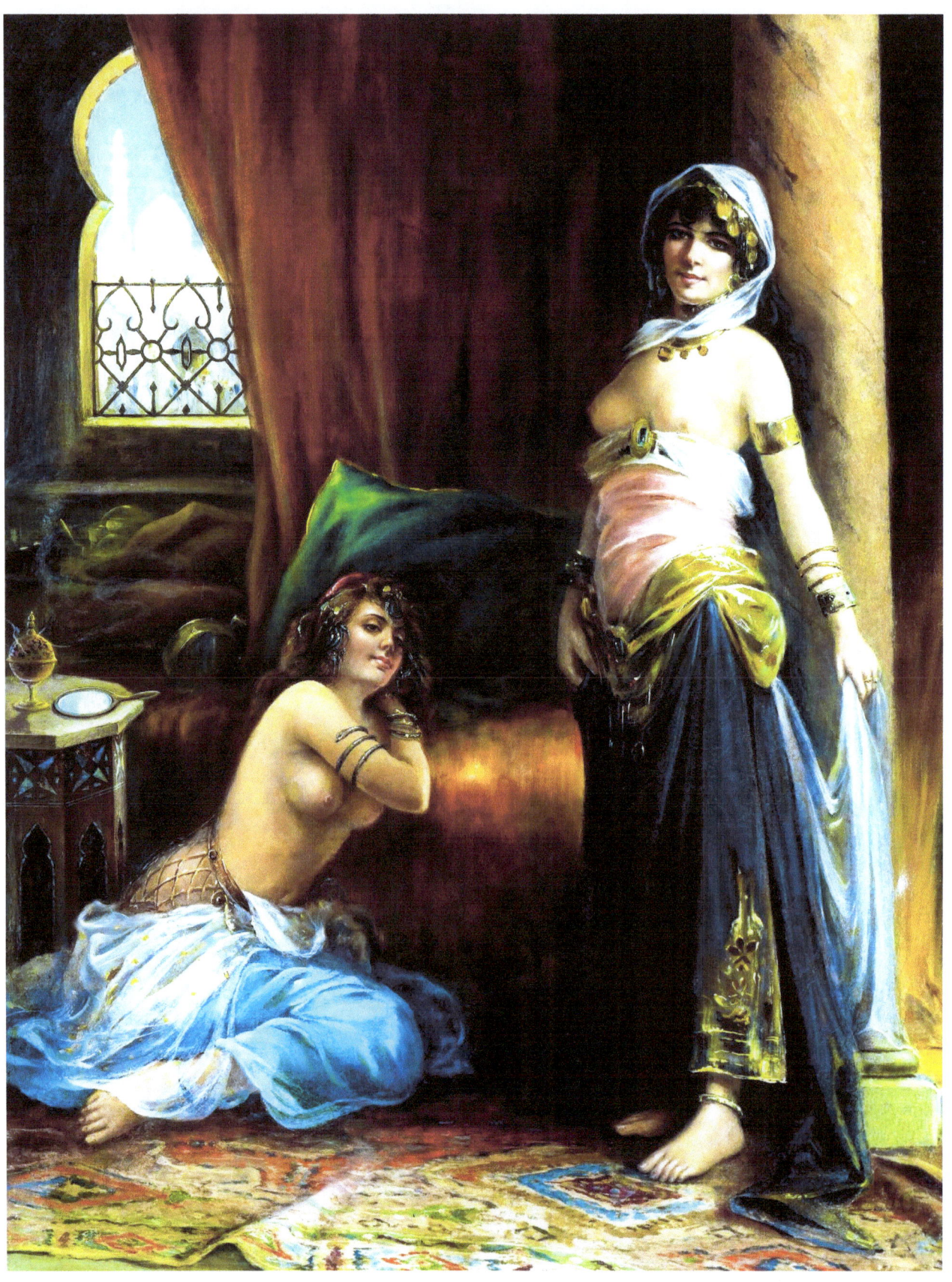

Nude on Blue Background by Ernst Kirchner

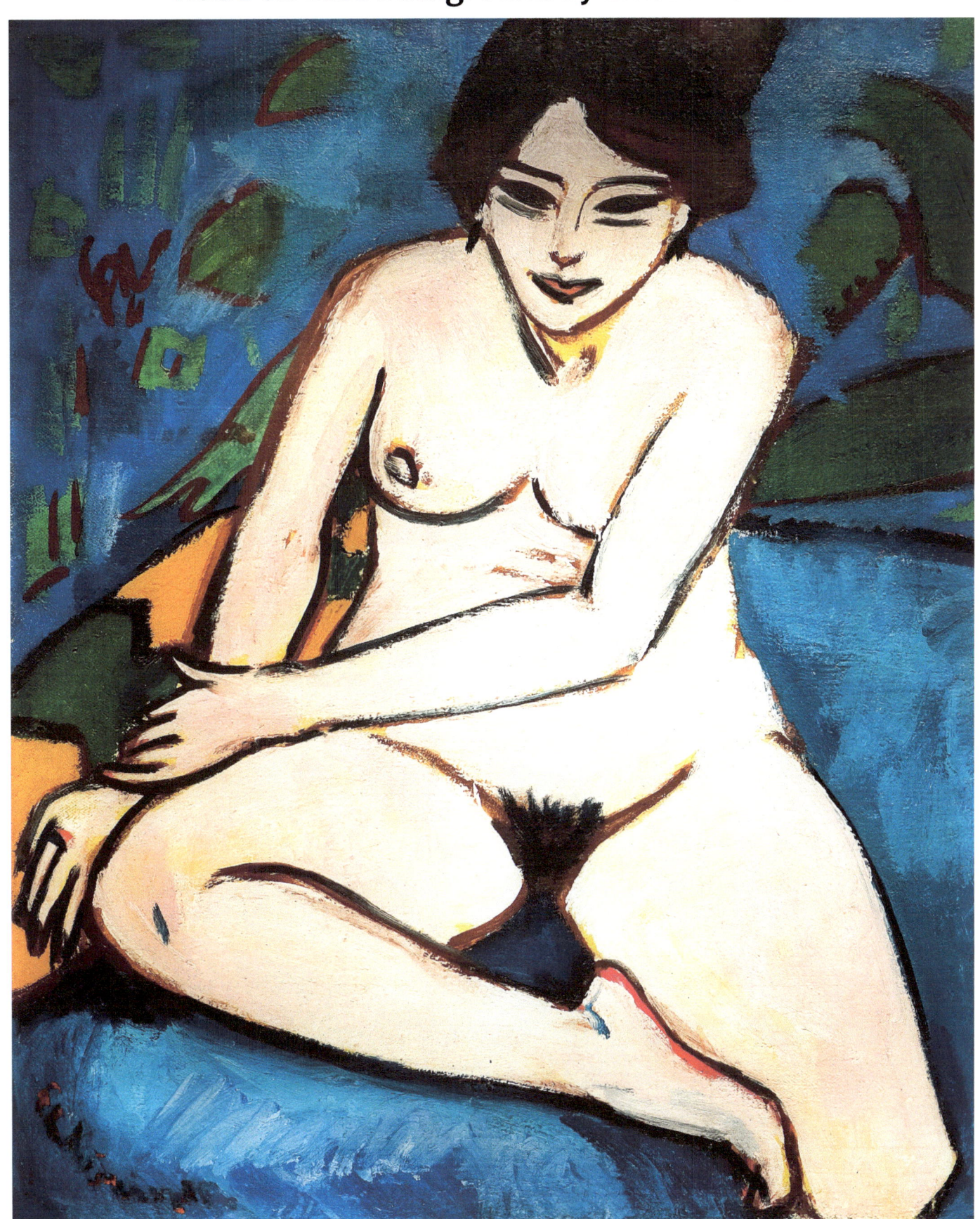

Nude Next to Radiator By Pierre Bonnard

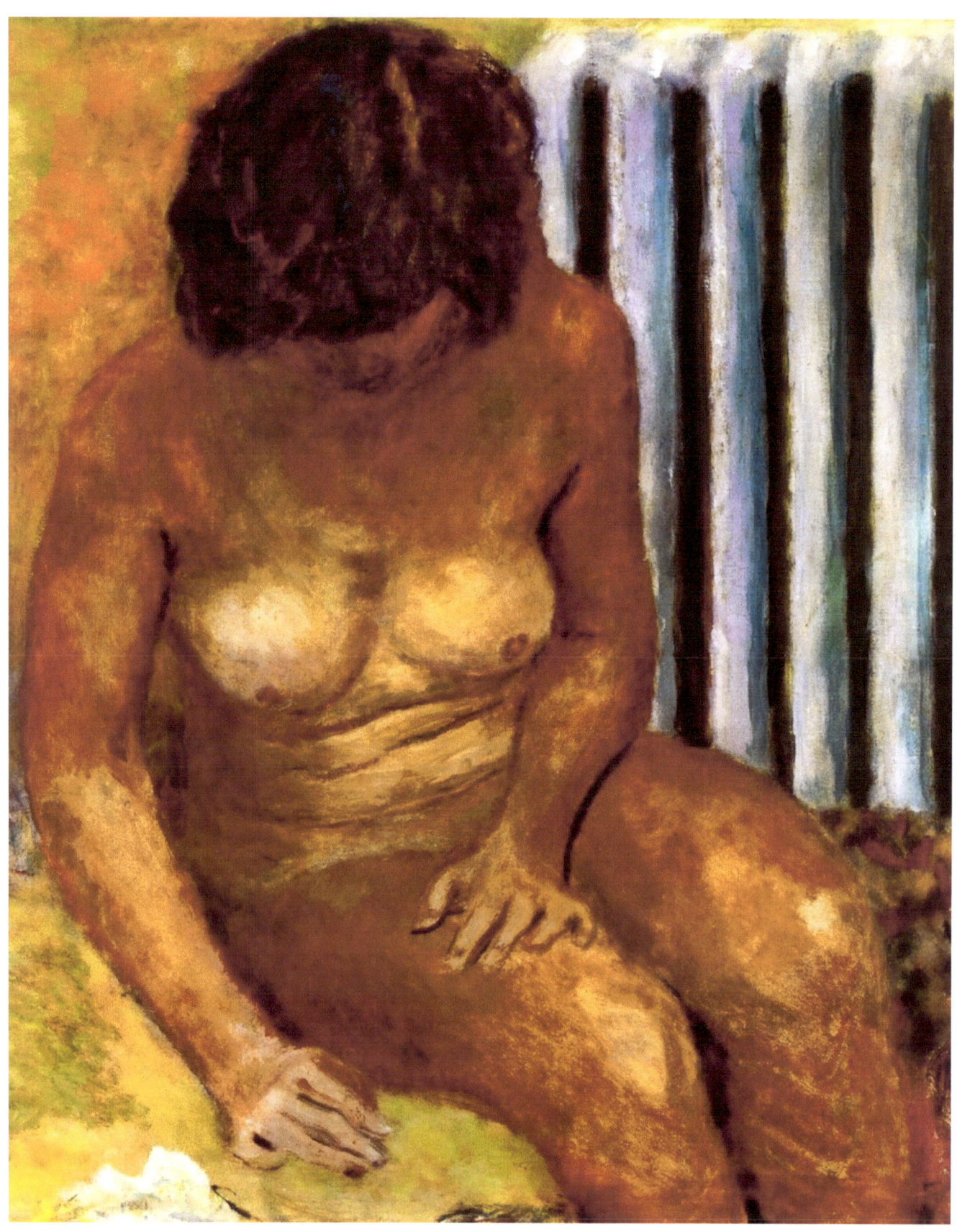

Eh? You're Jealous? by Paul Gauguin

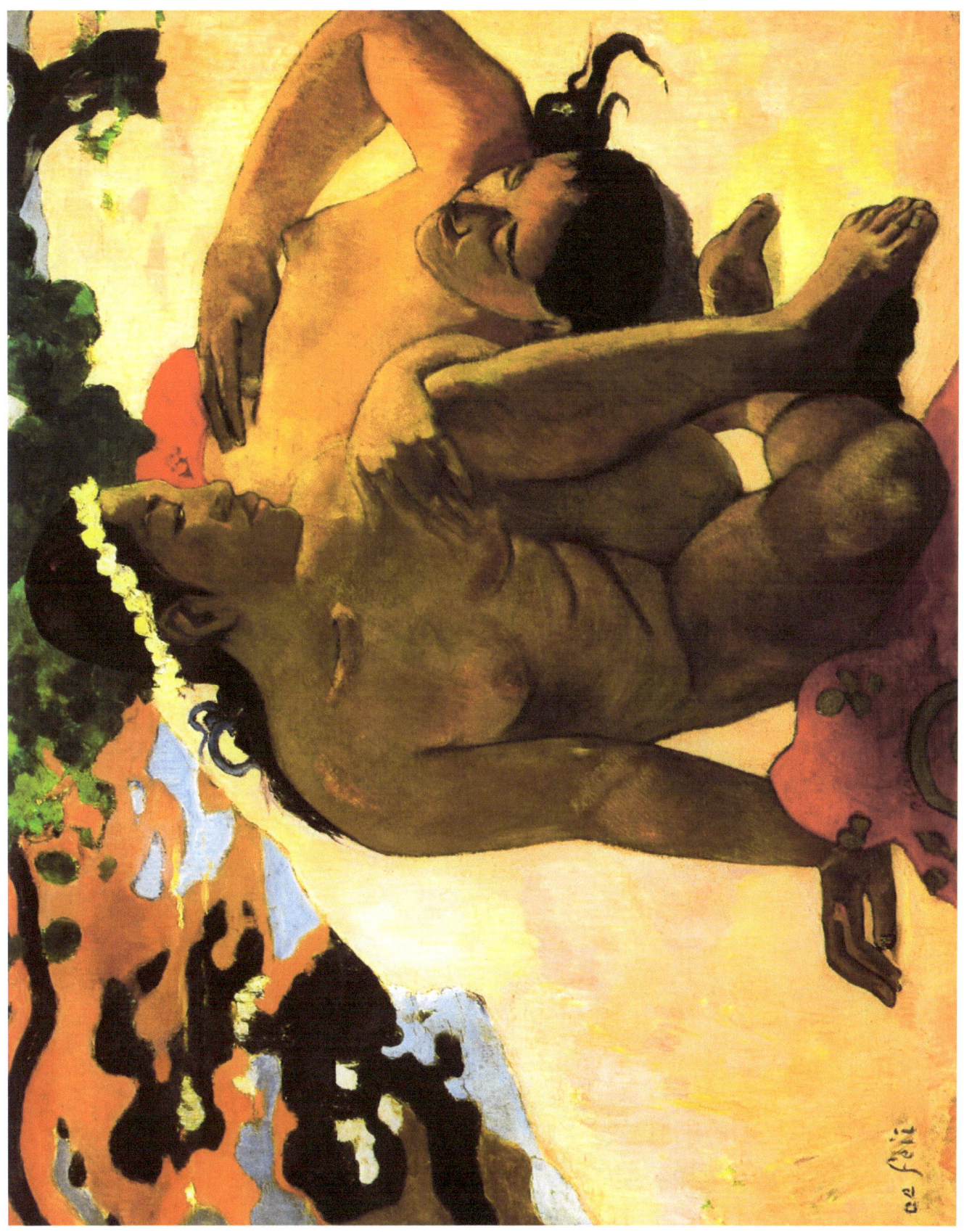

The Three Ages of Woman by Gustav Klimt

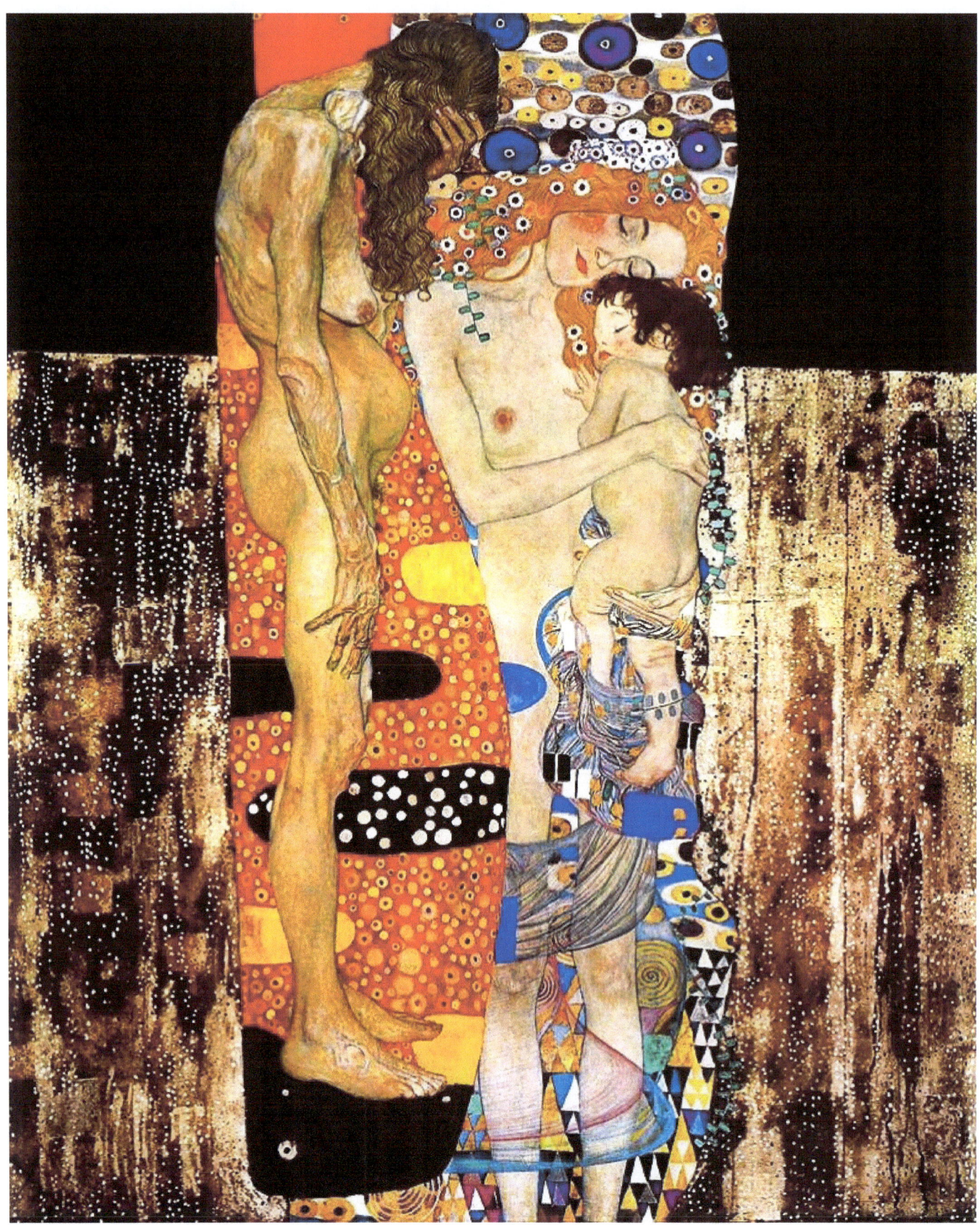

Nude Reclining on Sofa by Suzanne Valadon

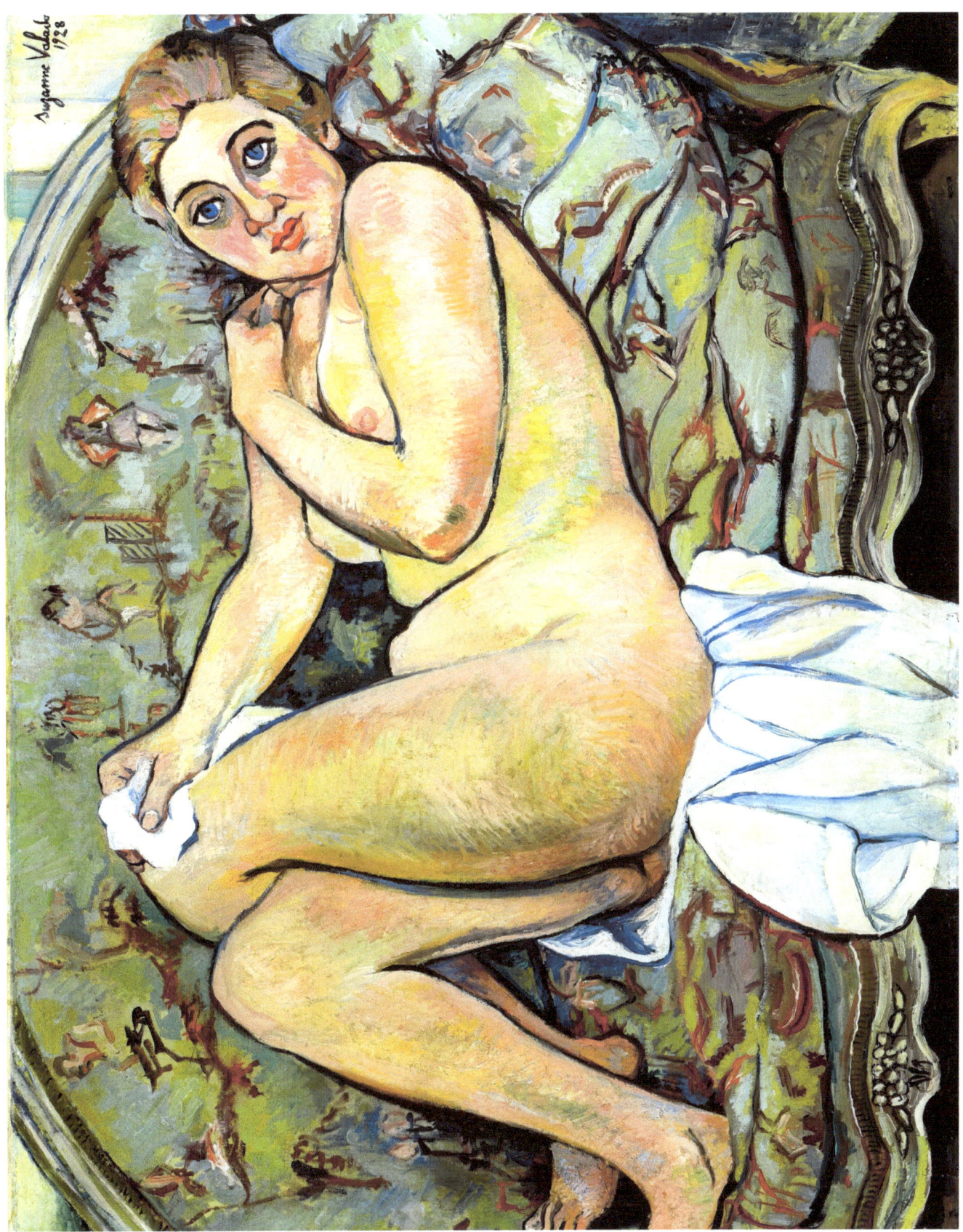

Nude in the Clouds – Cover from La Vie Parisian 1925

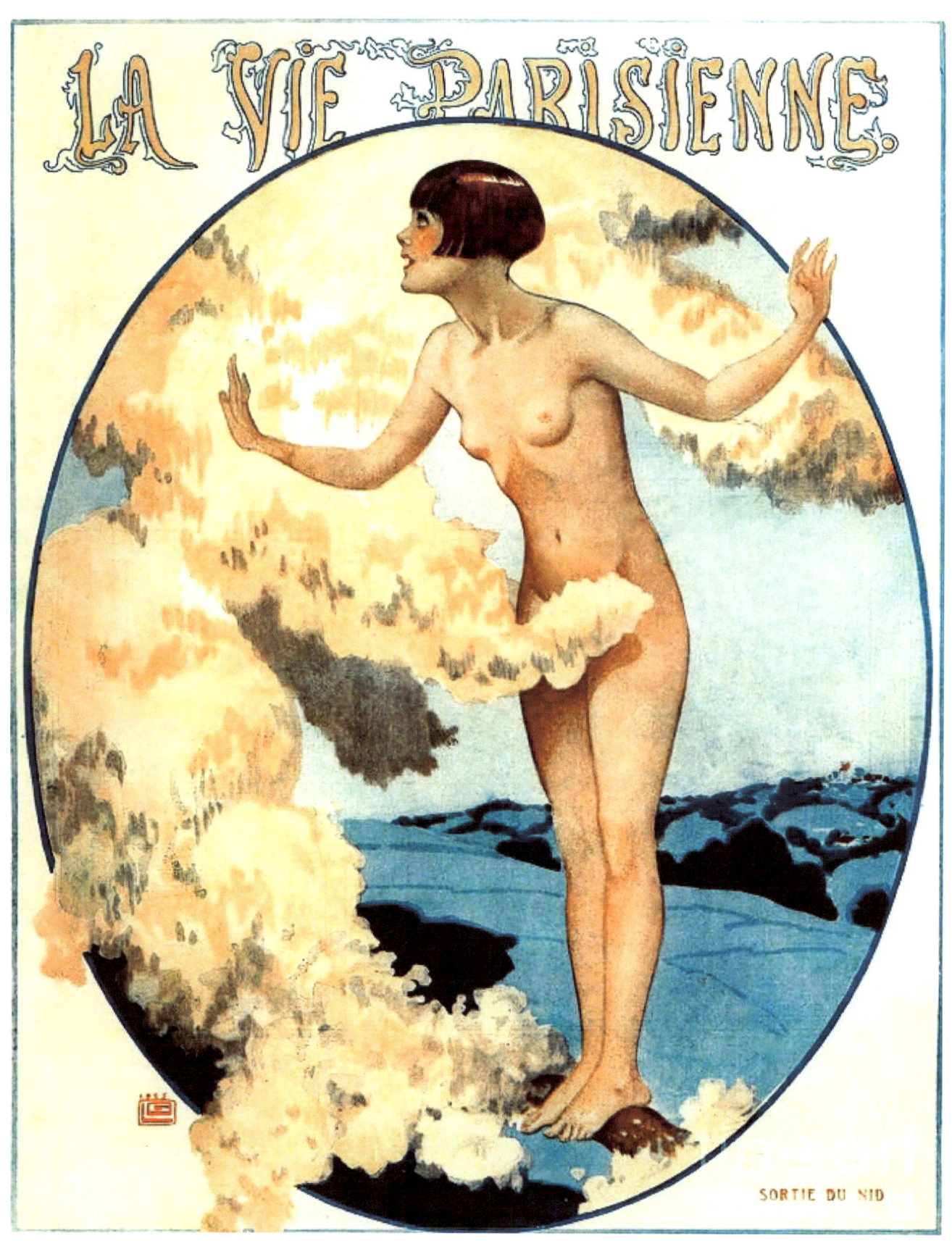

Two Nude Women by Water by Egon Schiele

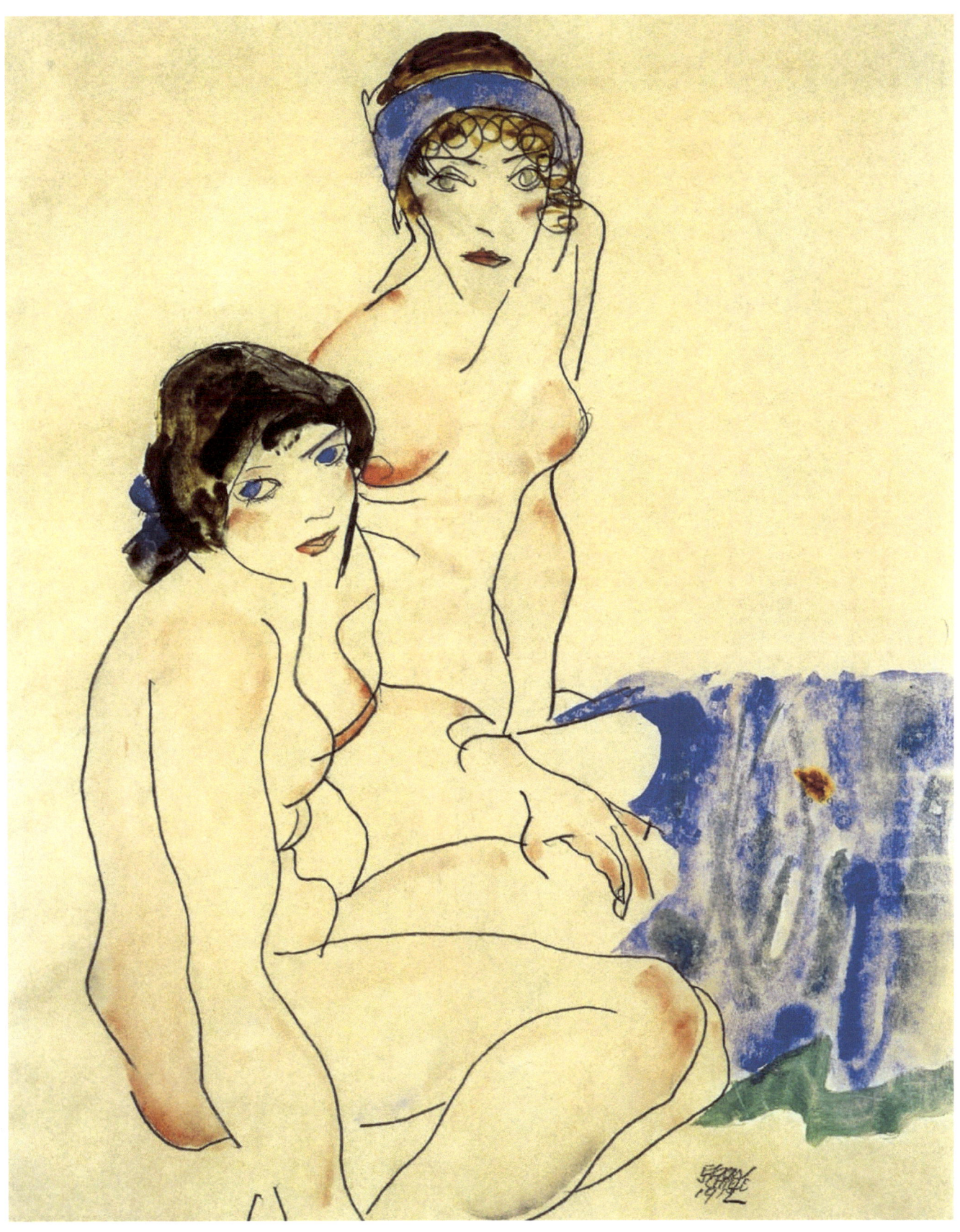

Nude Male Leaning Against Box by Gustav Klimt

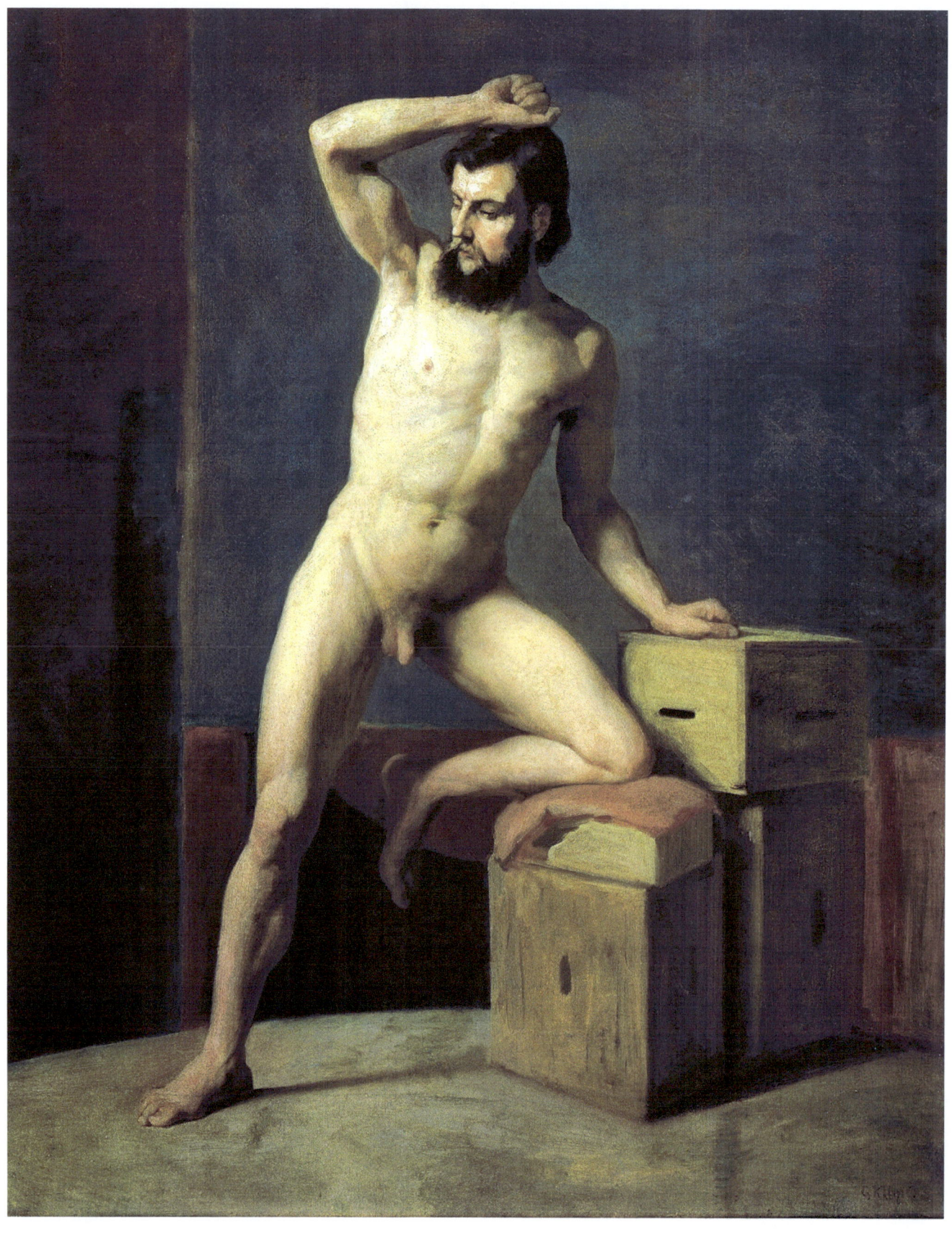

La Toilette by Frederic Bazille

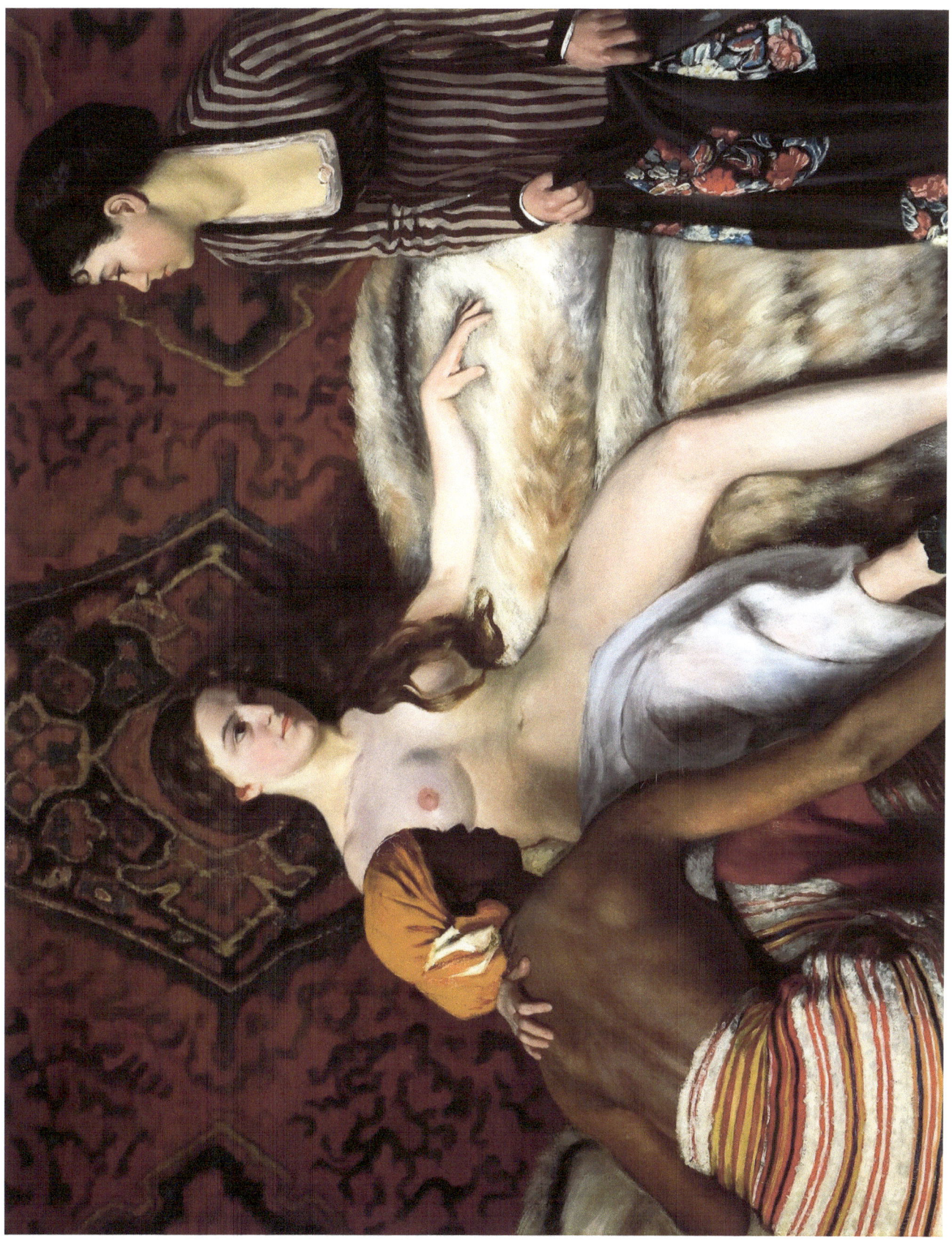

Three Mermaids, 1879 by Hans Thoma

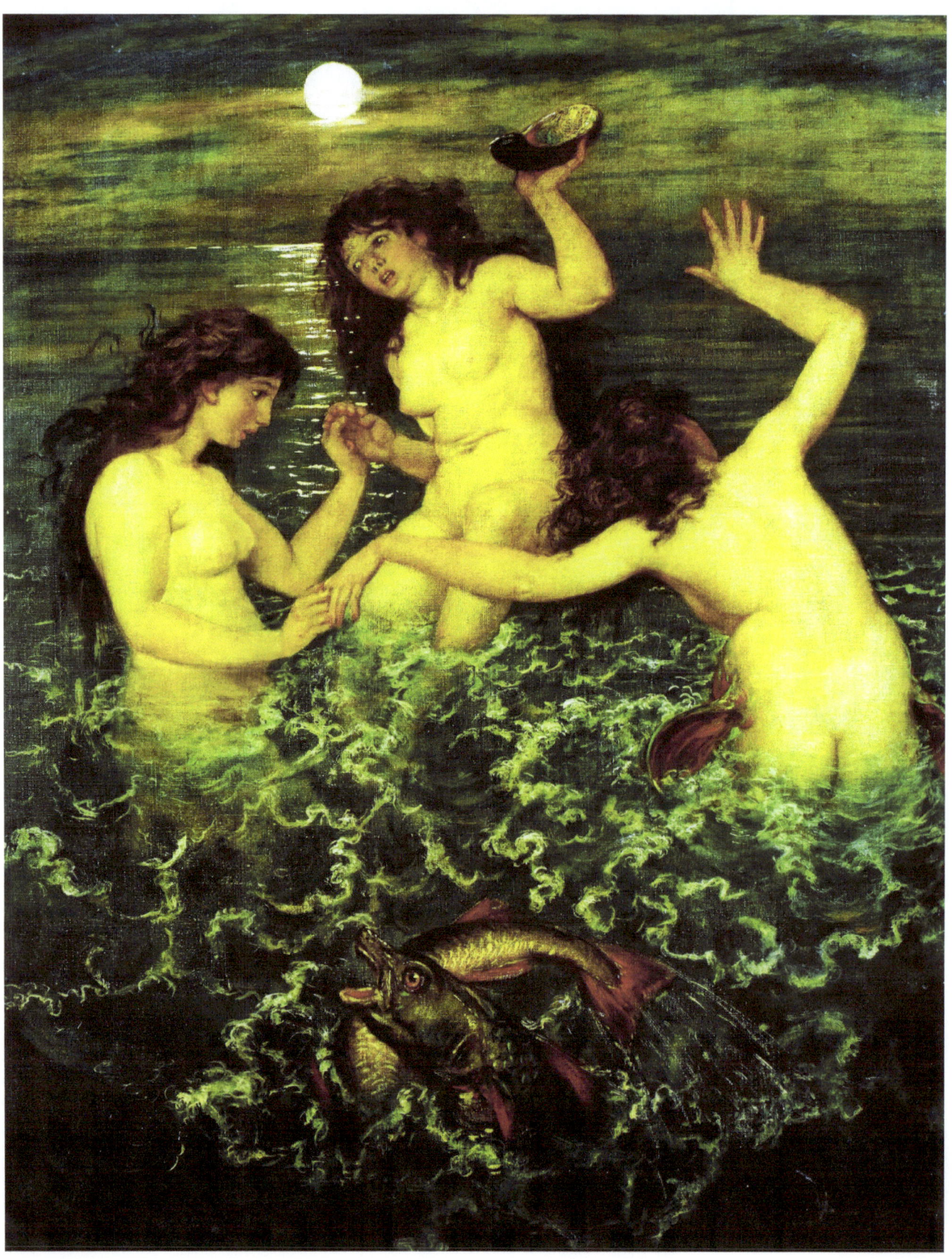

Morning in the City by Edward Hopper

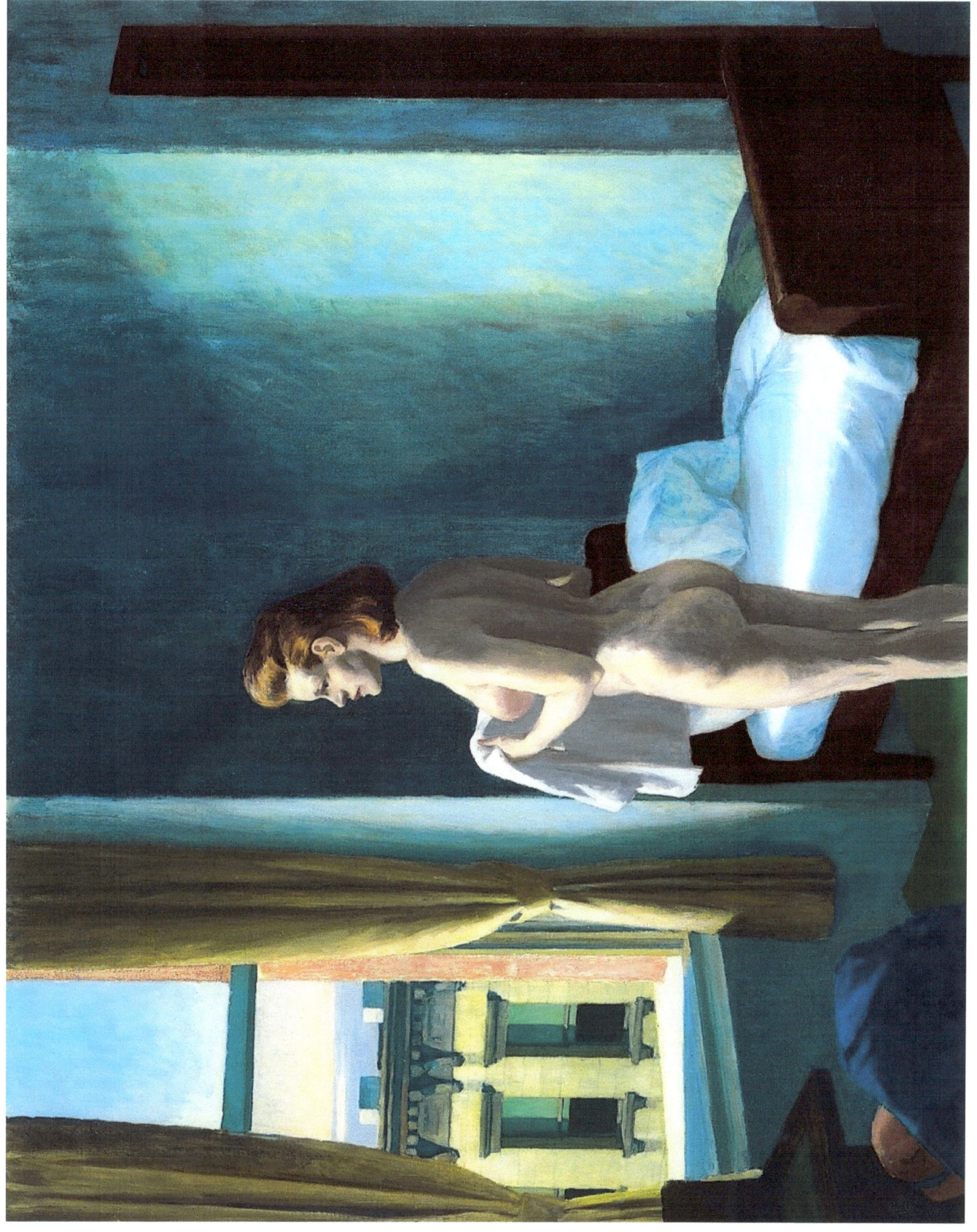

Nude Woman in Bed by Toulouse Lautrec

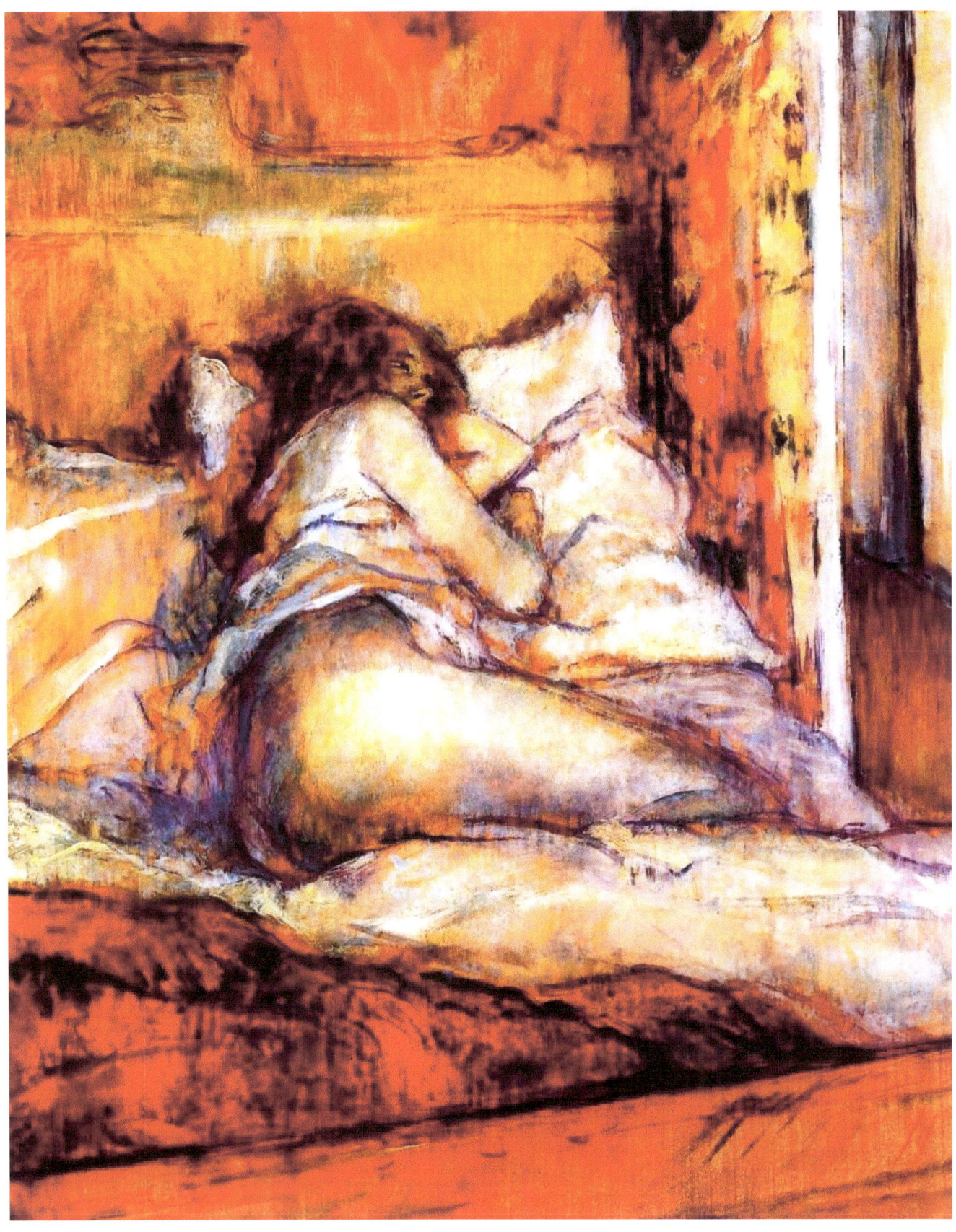

Nude Standing by Tikhov

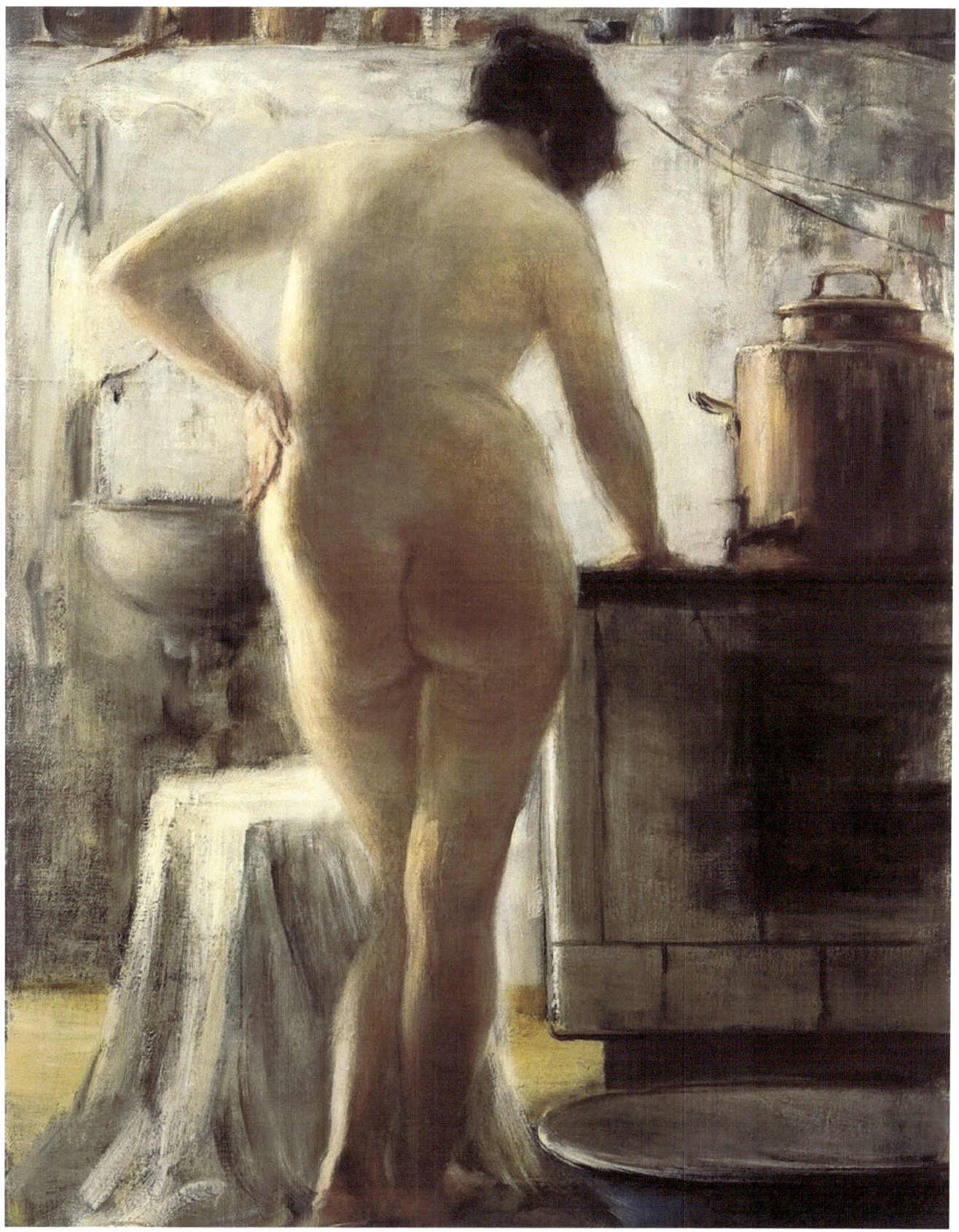

Bacchanale by Leo Putz

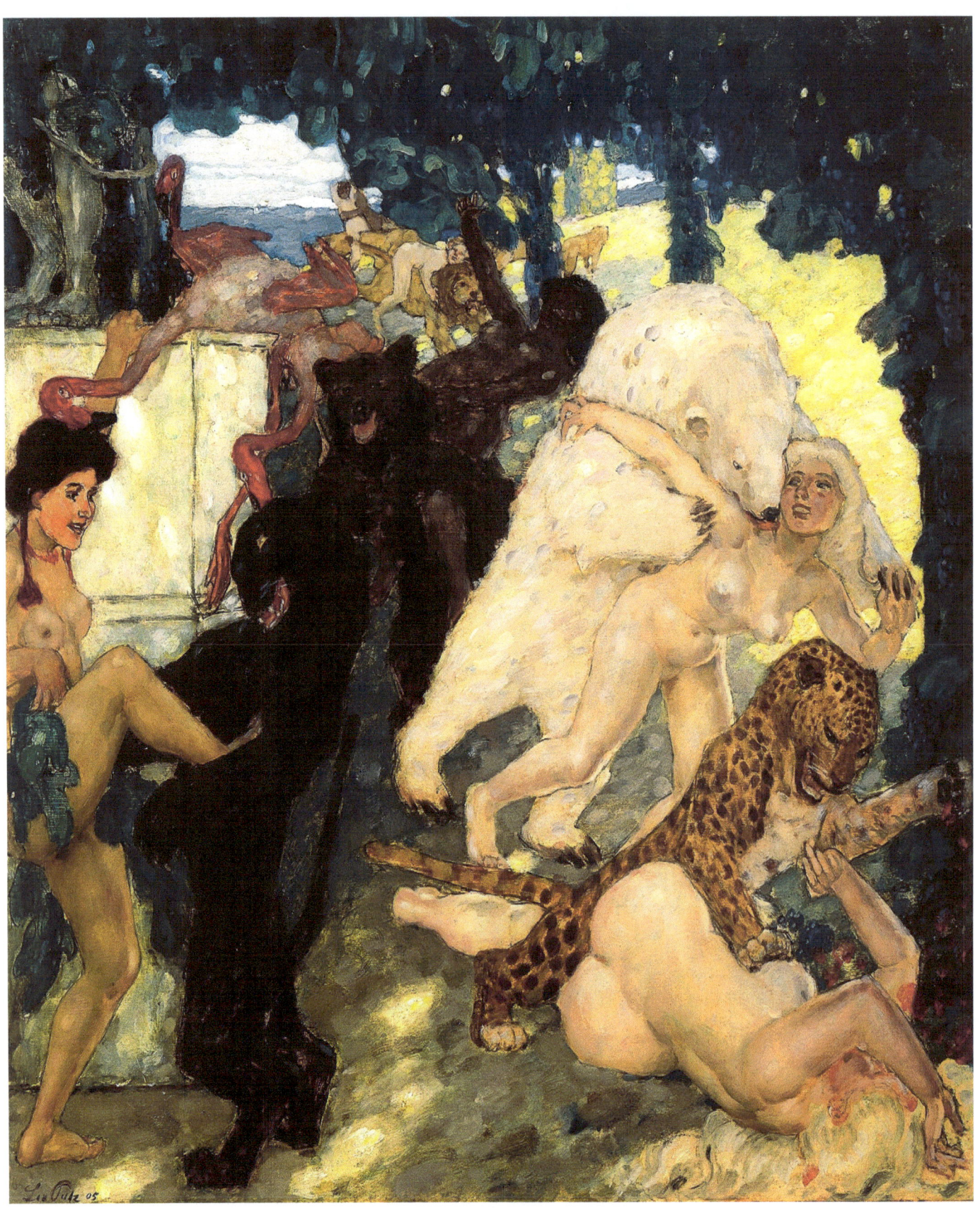

Sarah Bernhardt by Georges Antoine Rochegrosse

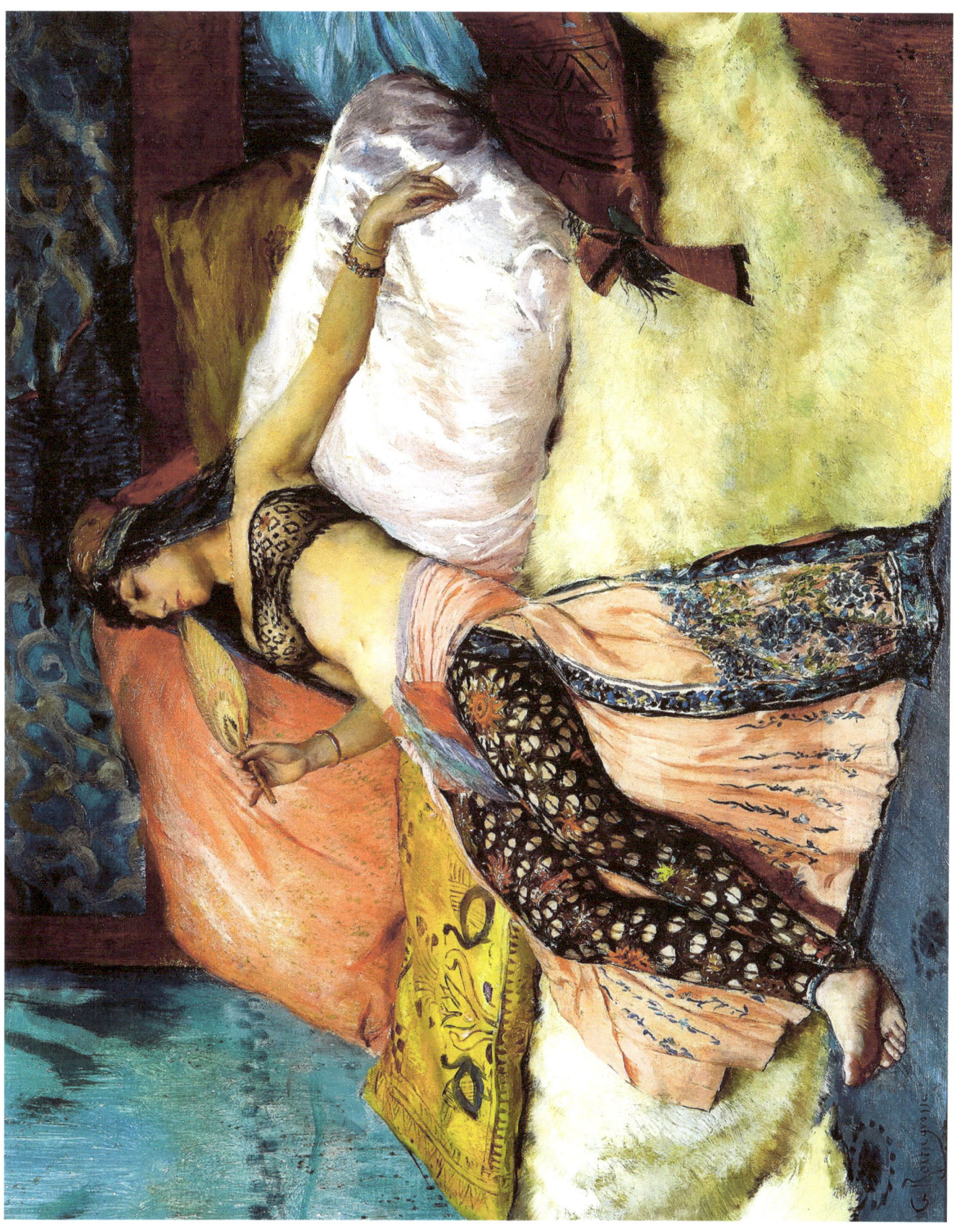

Orientalism - Nude Woman of the Harem by Gyula Tornai

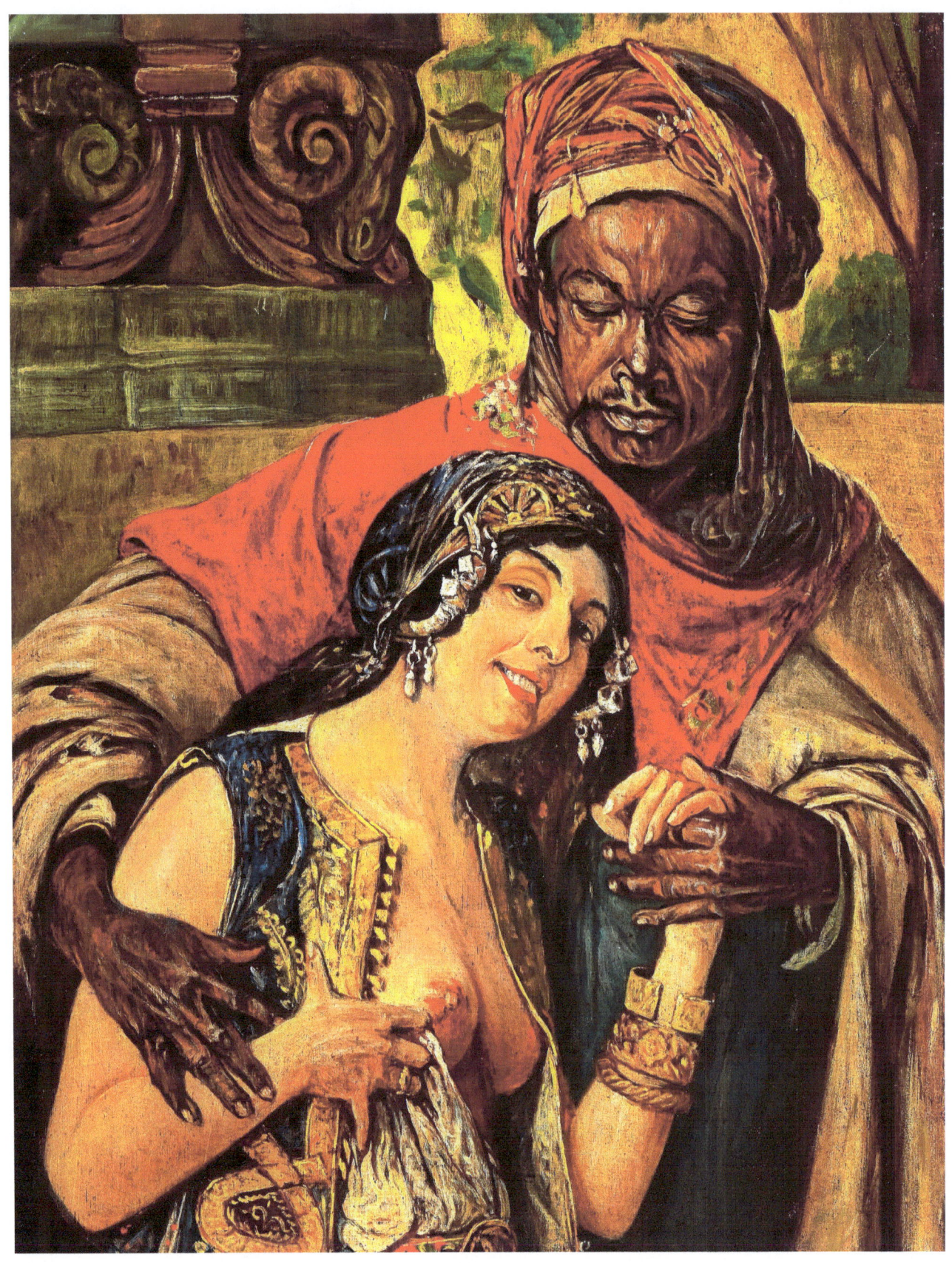

Nightclub Singer 1901 by Pablo Picasso

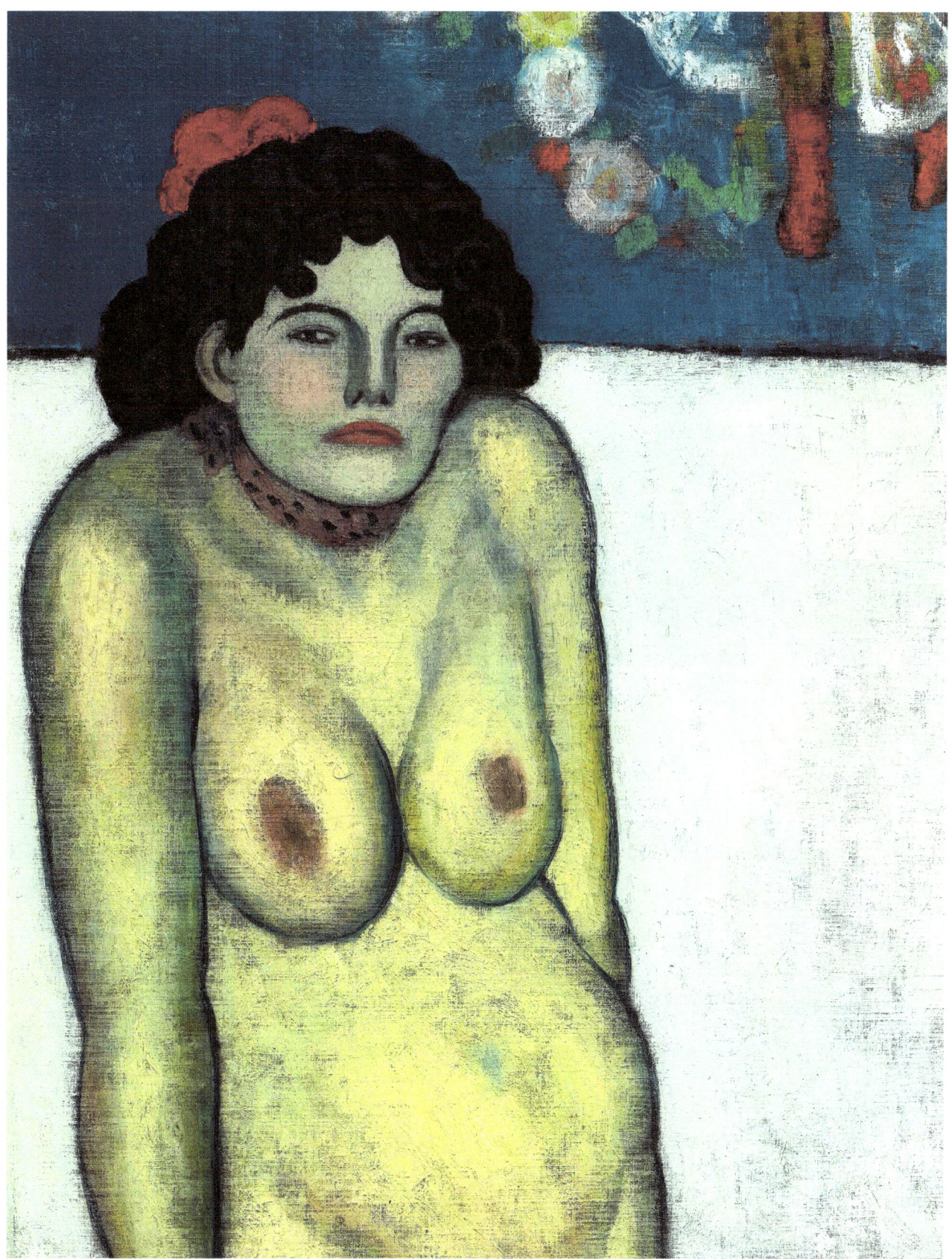

Two Women by Felix Vallotton

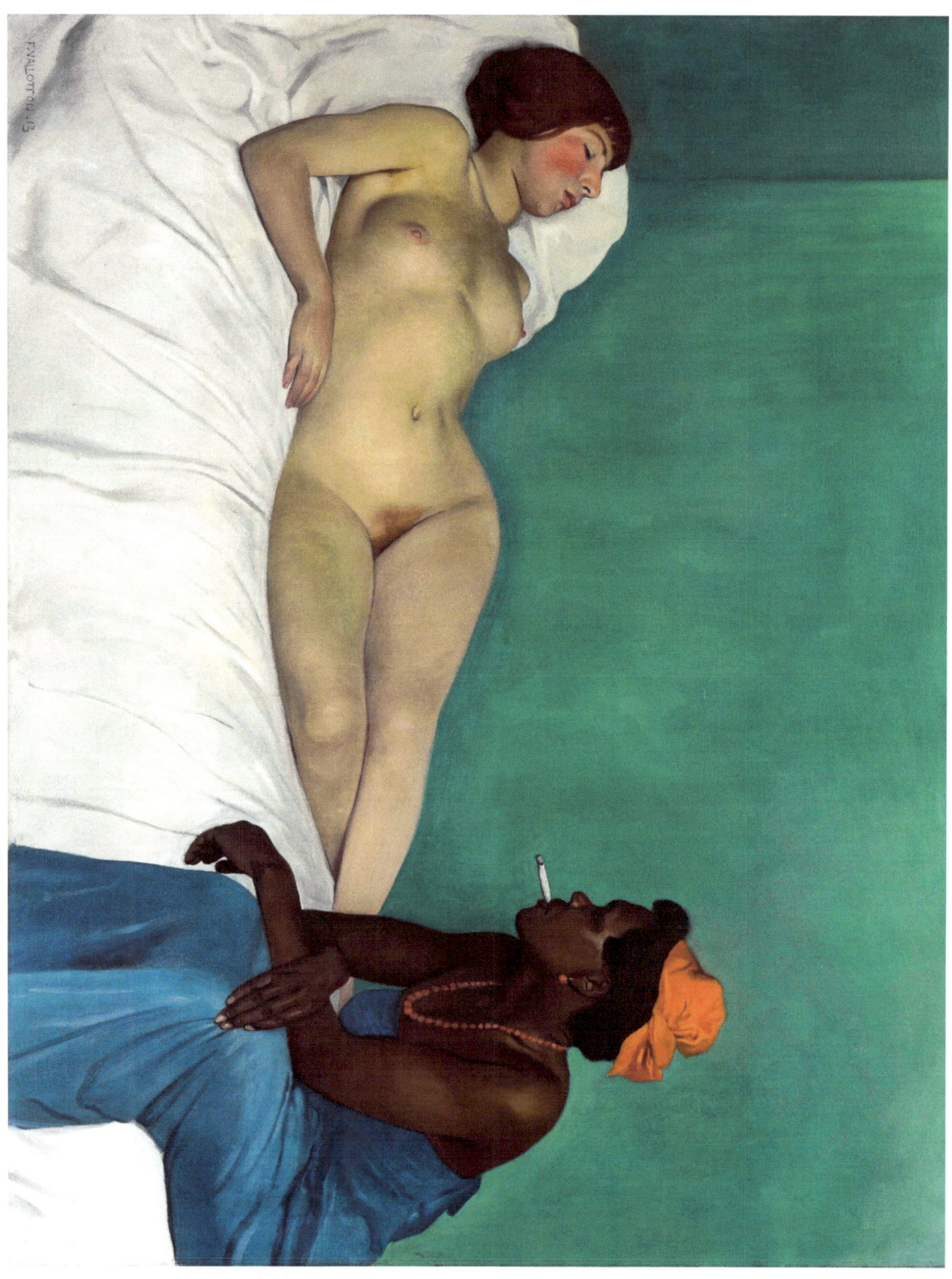

Portrait of Simonetta Vespucci 1480 by Piero di Cosimo

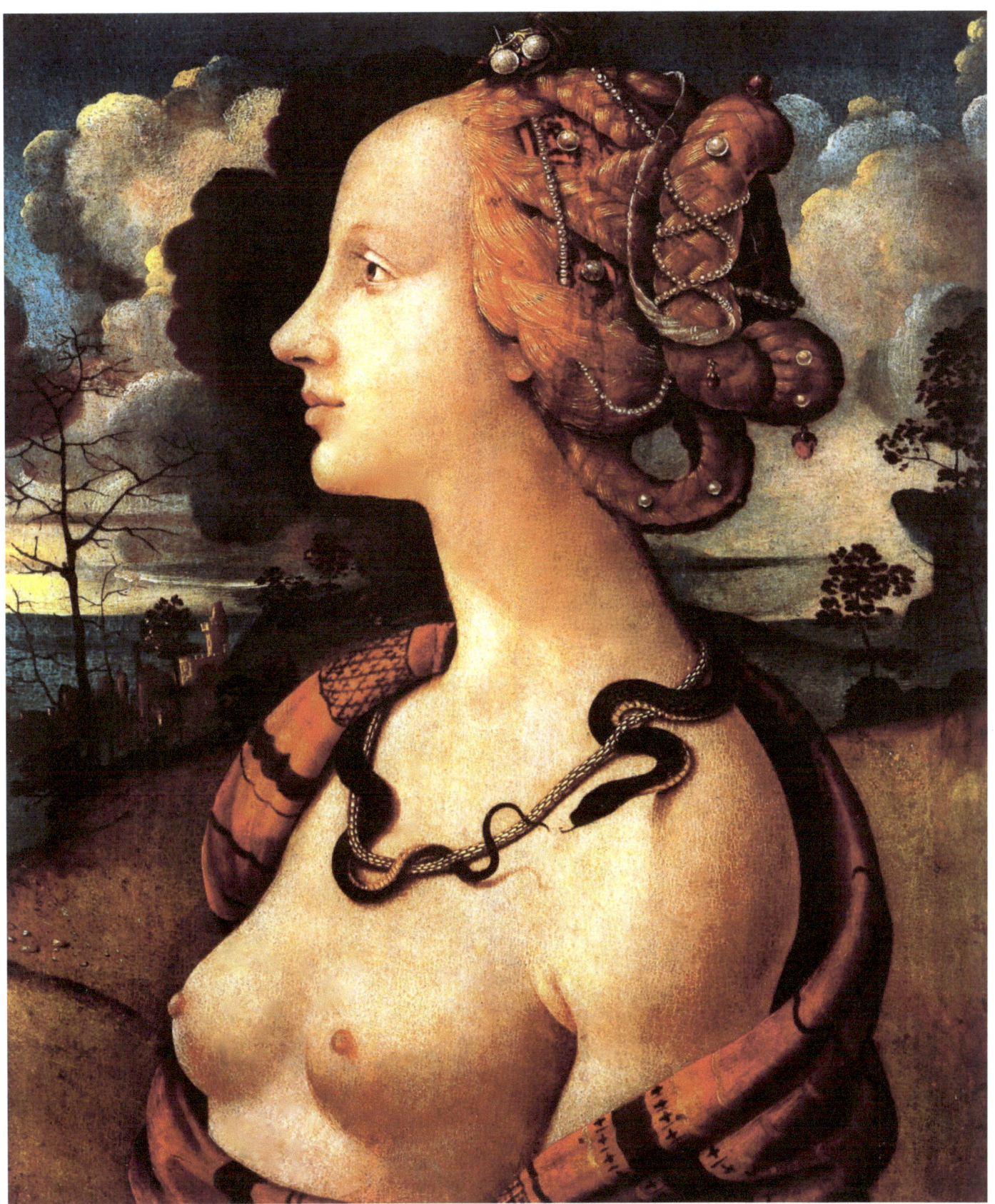

Odalisque by Georges Rochegrosse

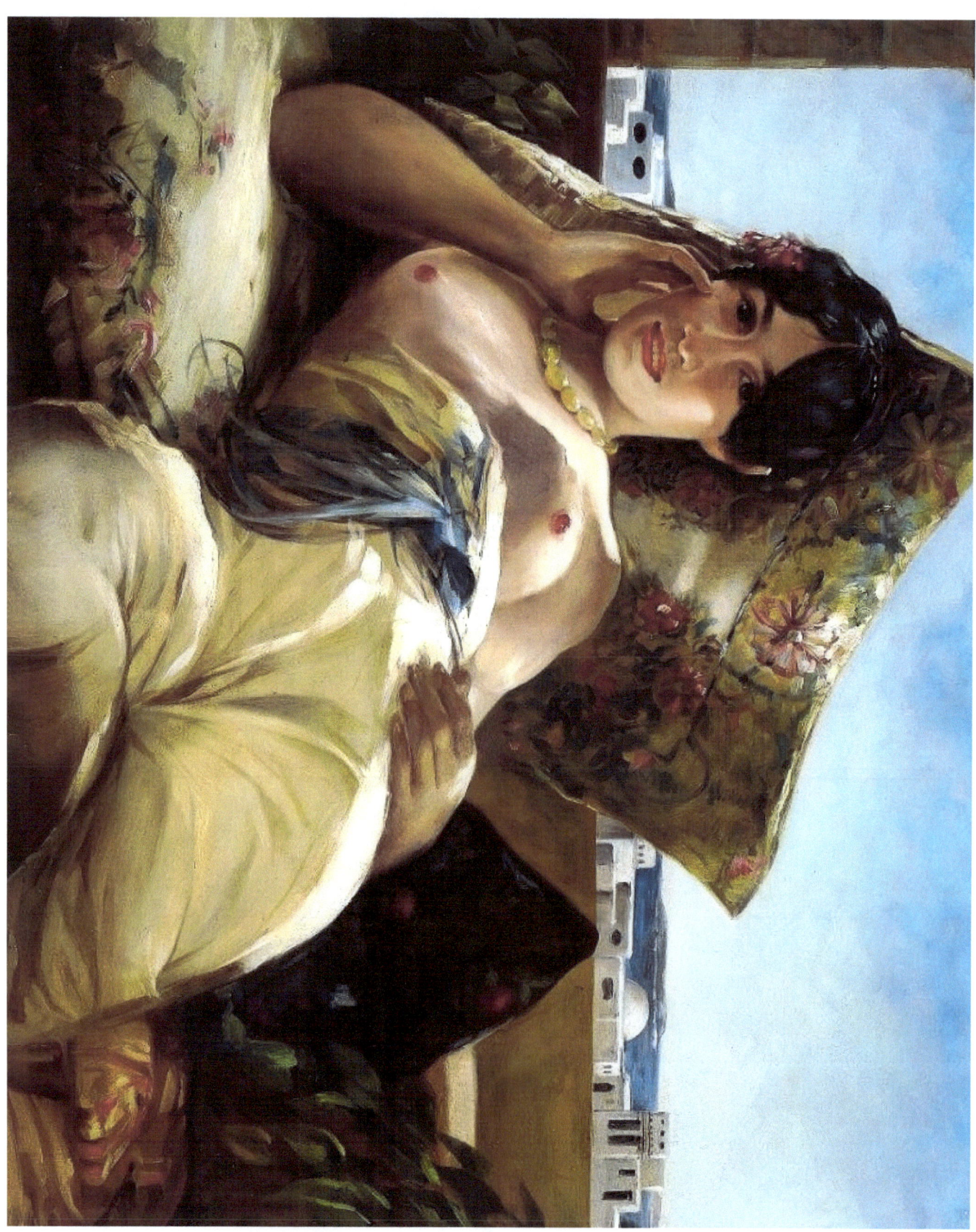

Underwater Kingdom by Ilya Repin

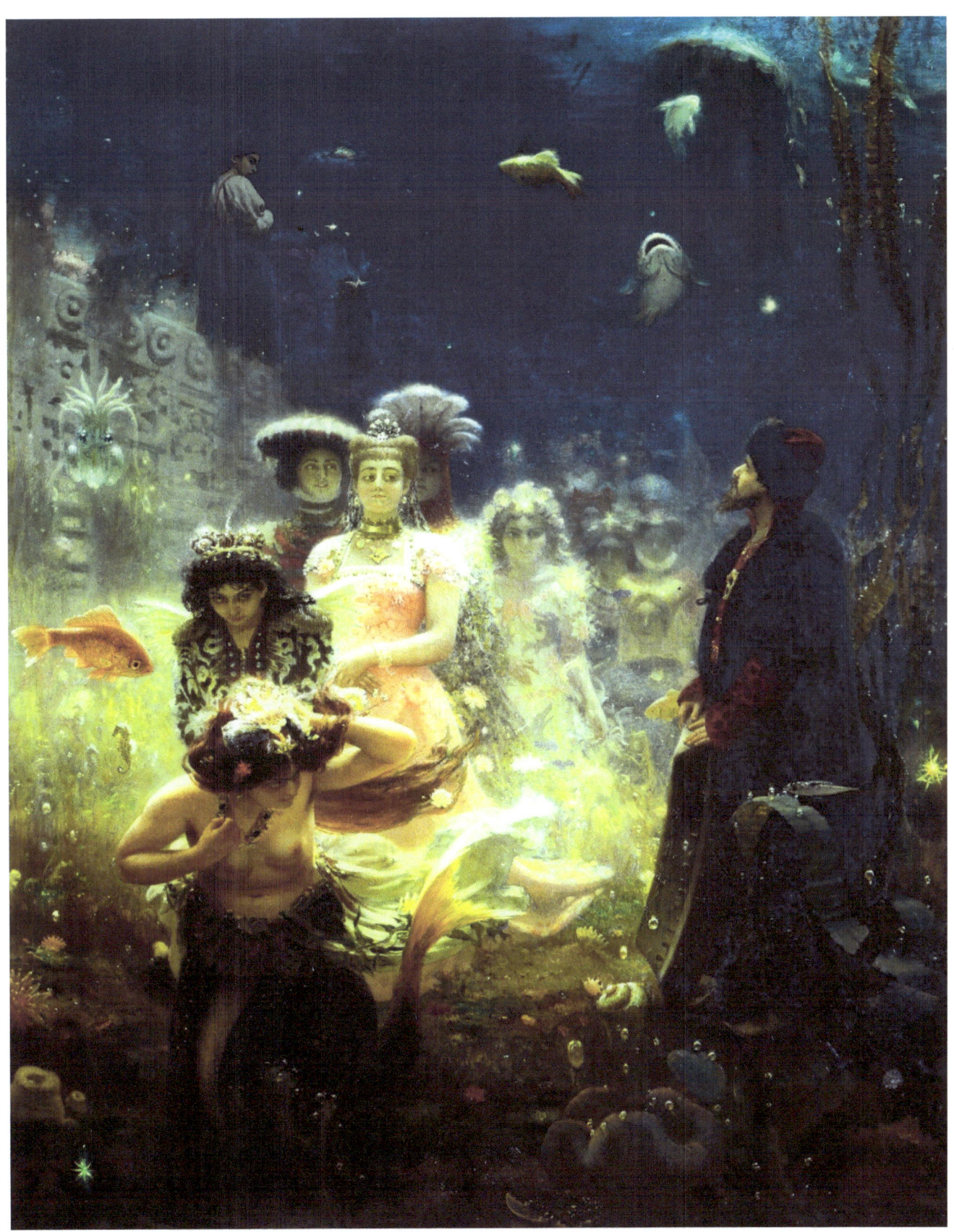

Antiope and Jupiter in the Form of a Satyr by Hendrick Goltzius

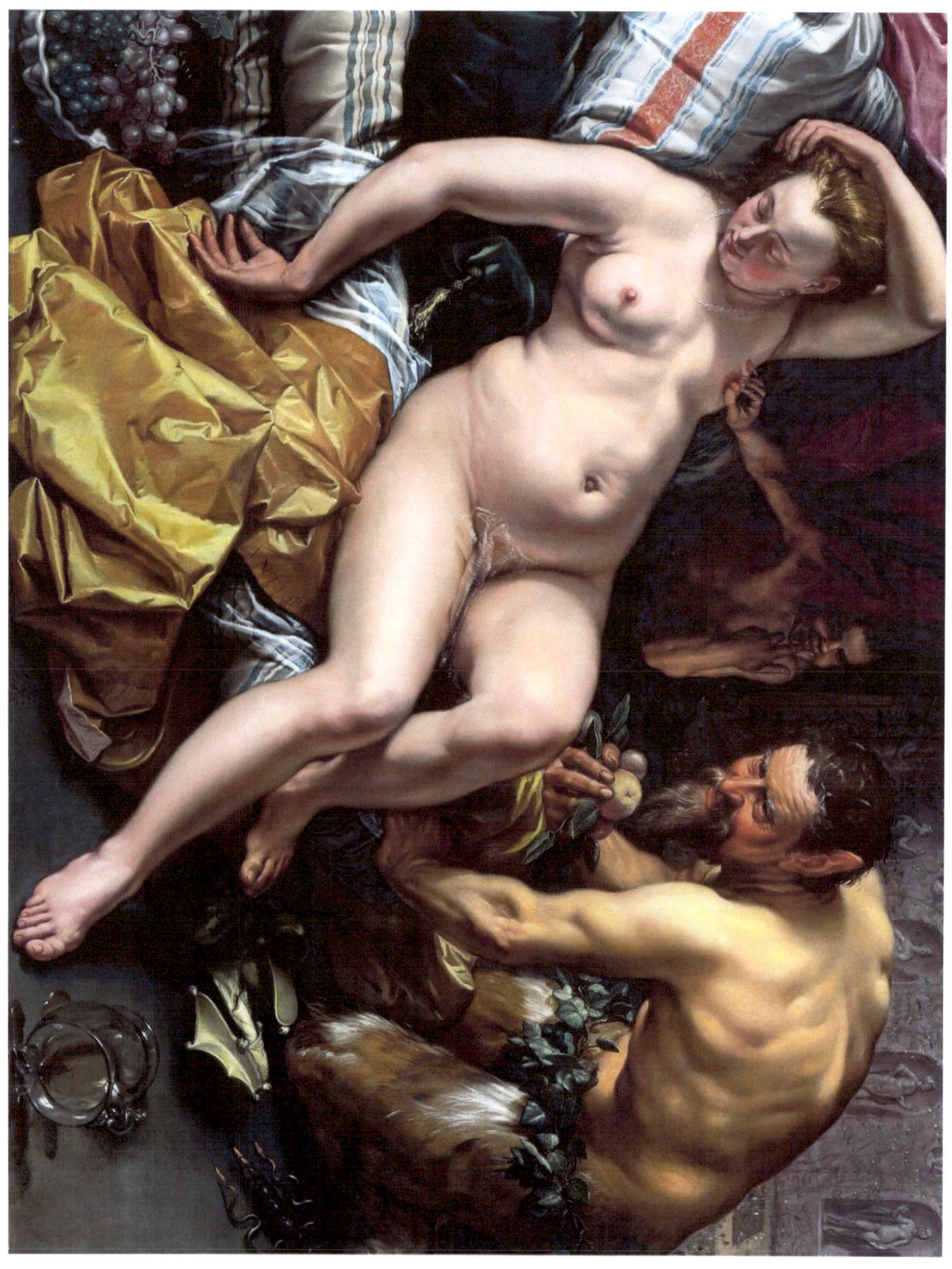

Ancient Roman Slave by Oscar Pereira da Silva

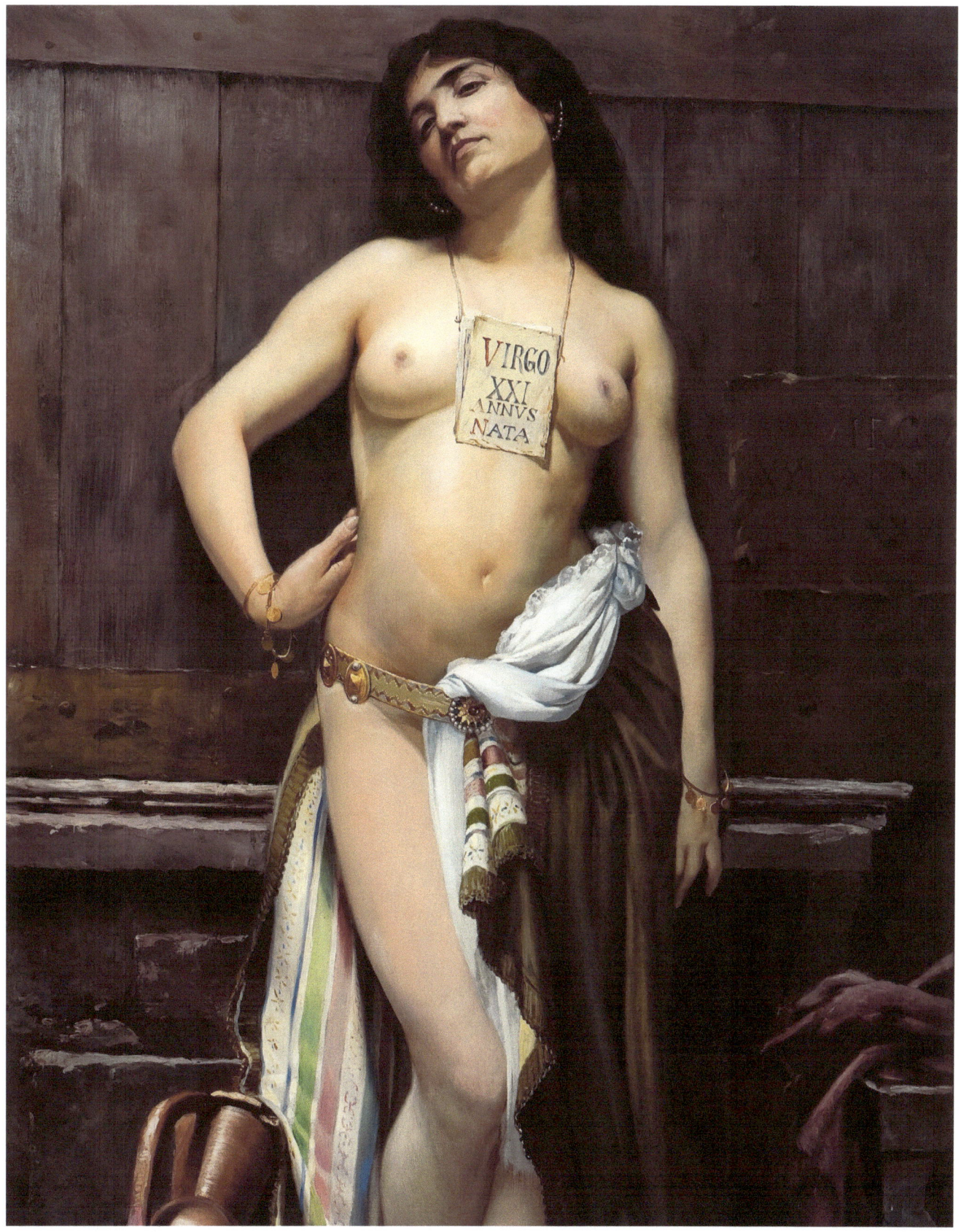

Nude Woman Miss Leslie Hall by George Bellows

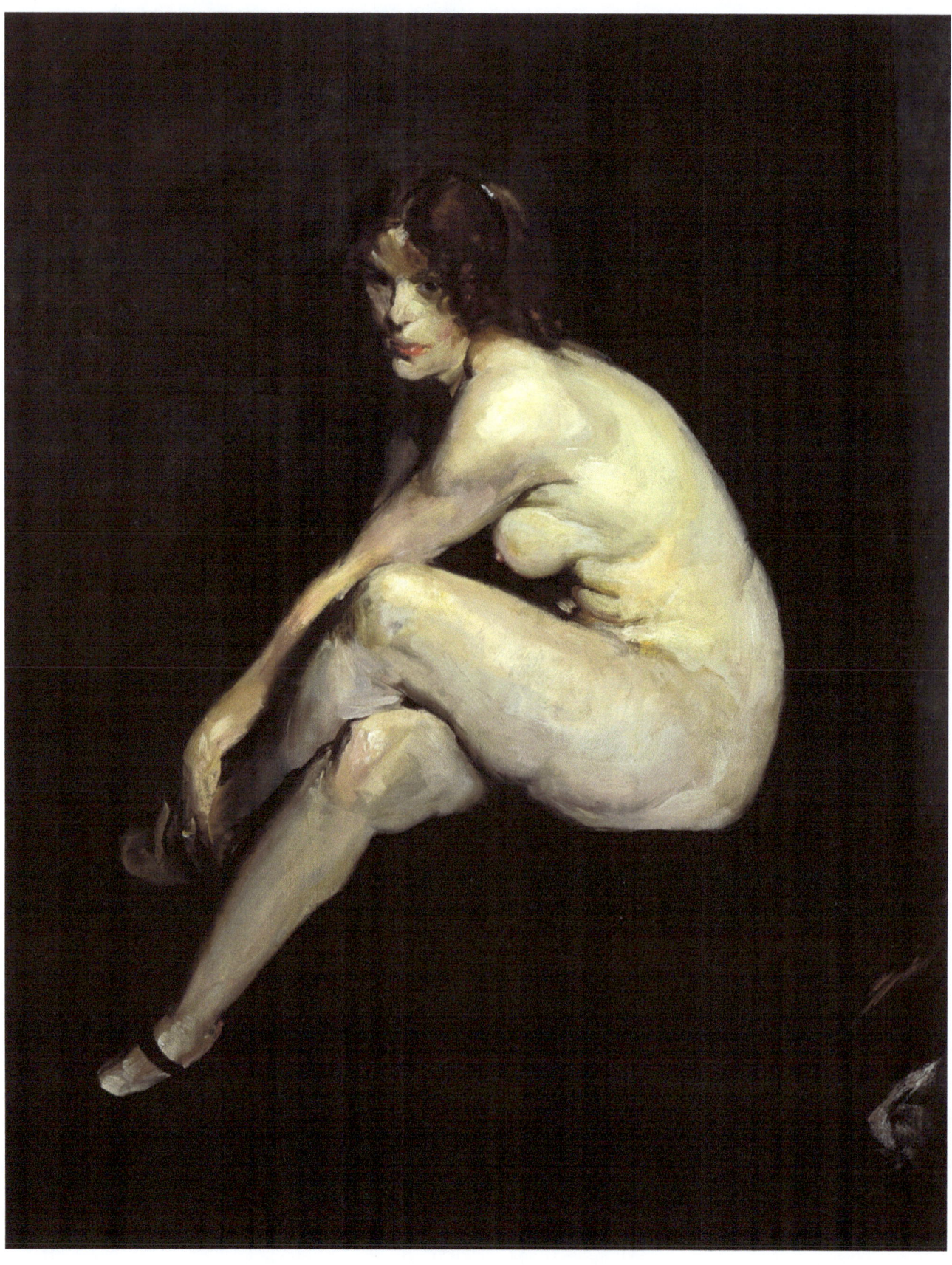

Bloodthirsty Erynnies Demon Vampires by Gustave Dore

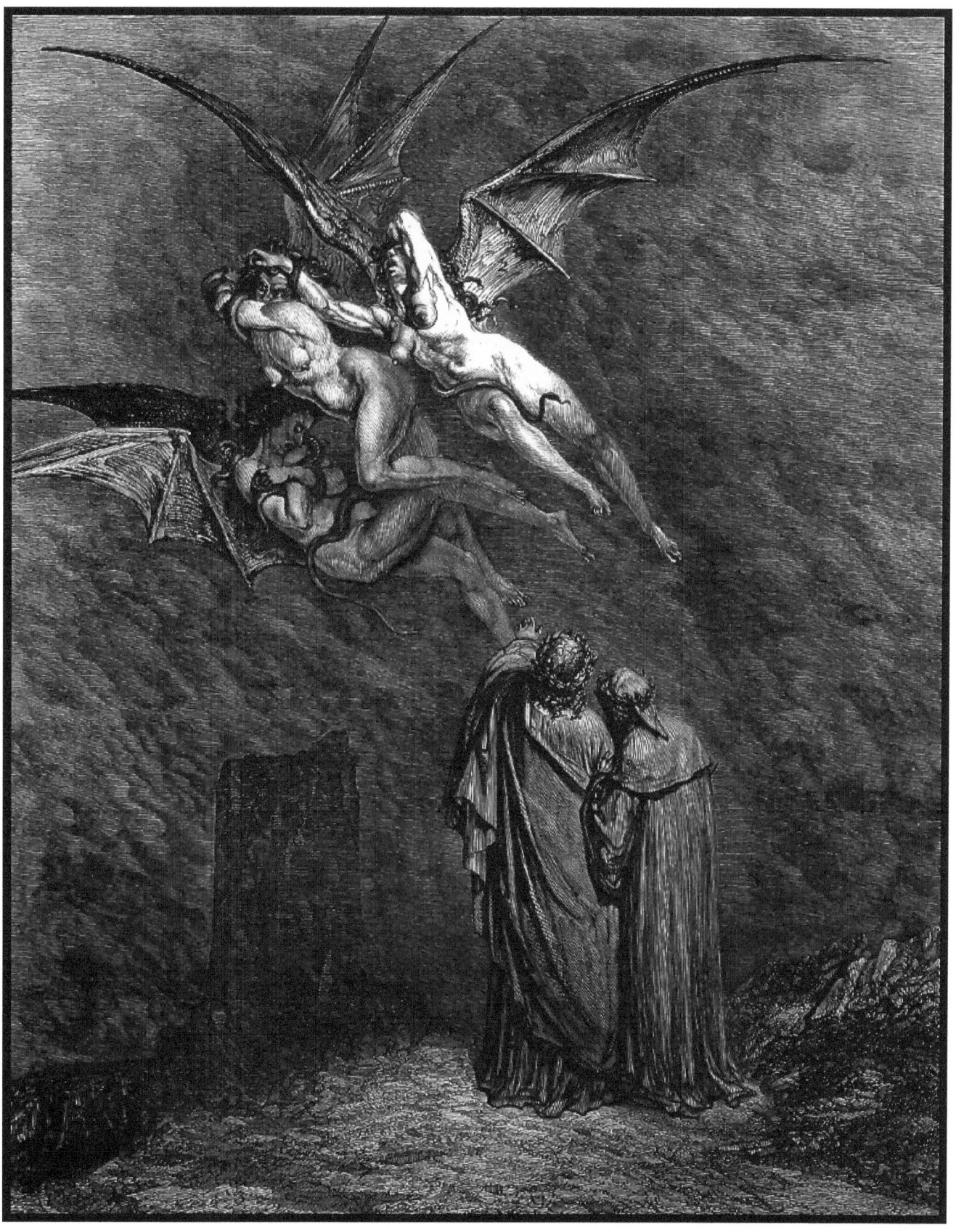

The Nude by Henri Lebasque

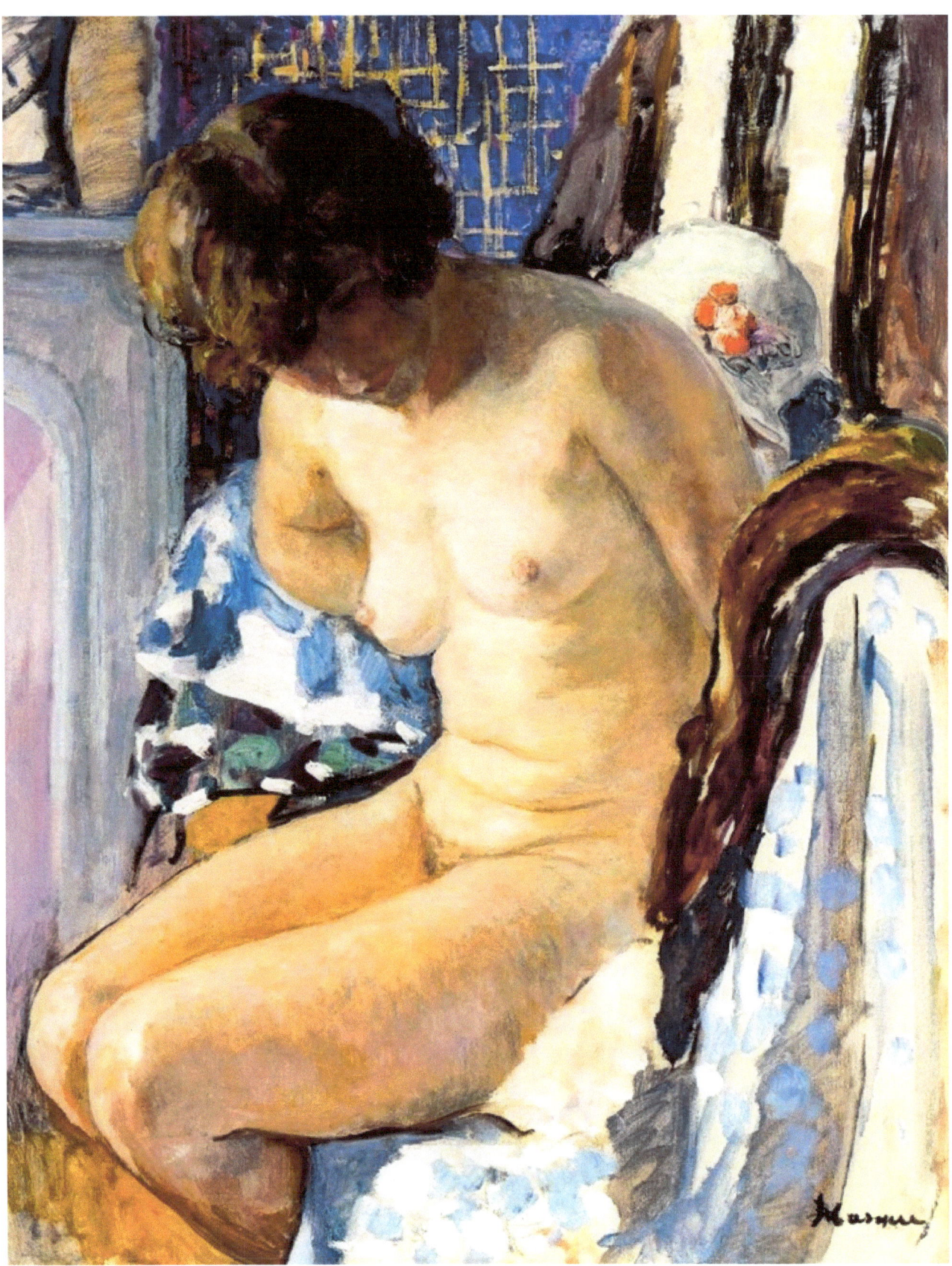

In a Russian Banya by Vitaly Tikhov

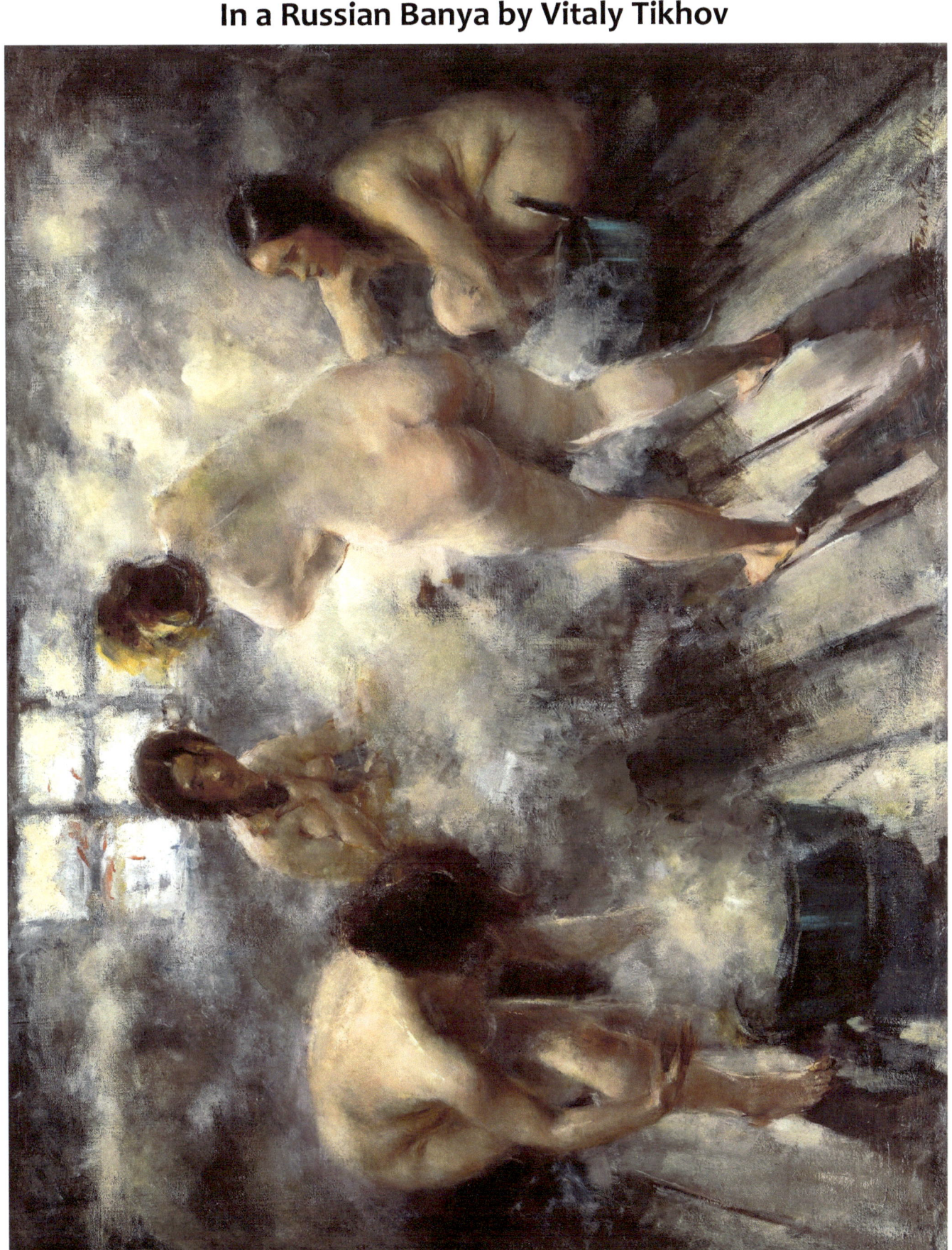

Nude Woman Unmasked by Akseli Gallen-Kallela

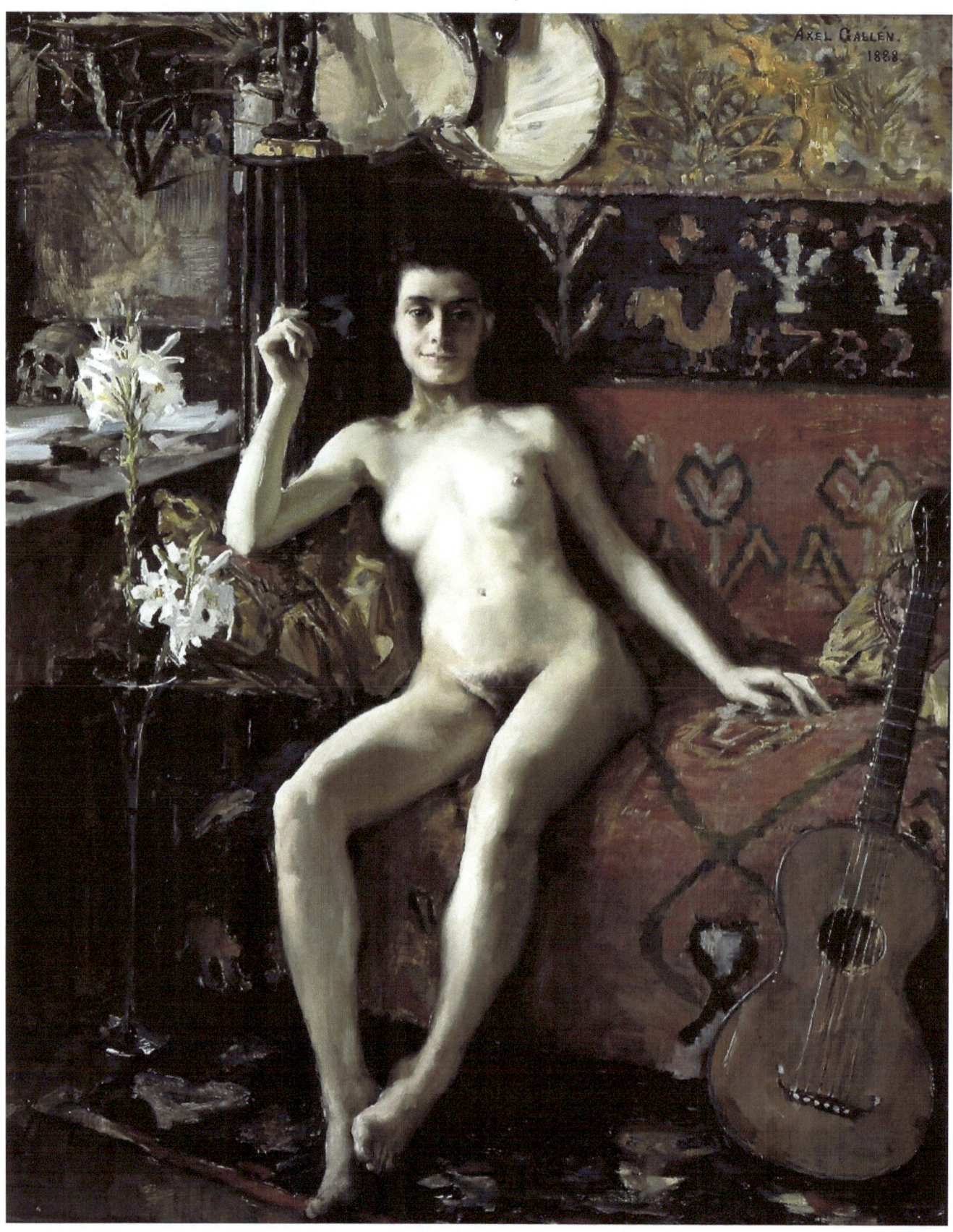

Nude on a Spring Morning by Henri Lebasque

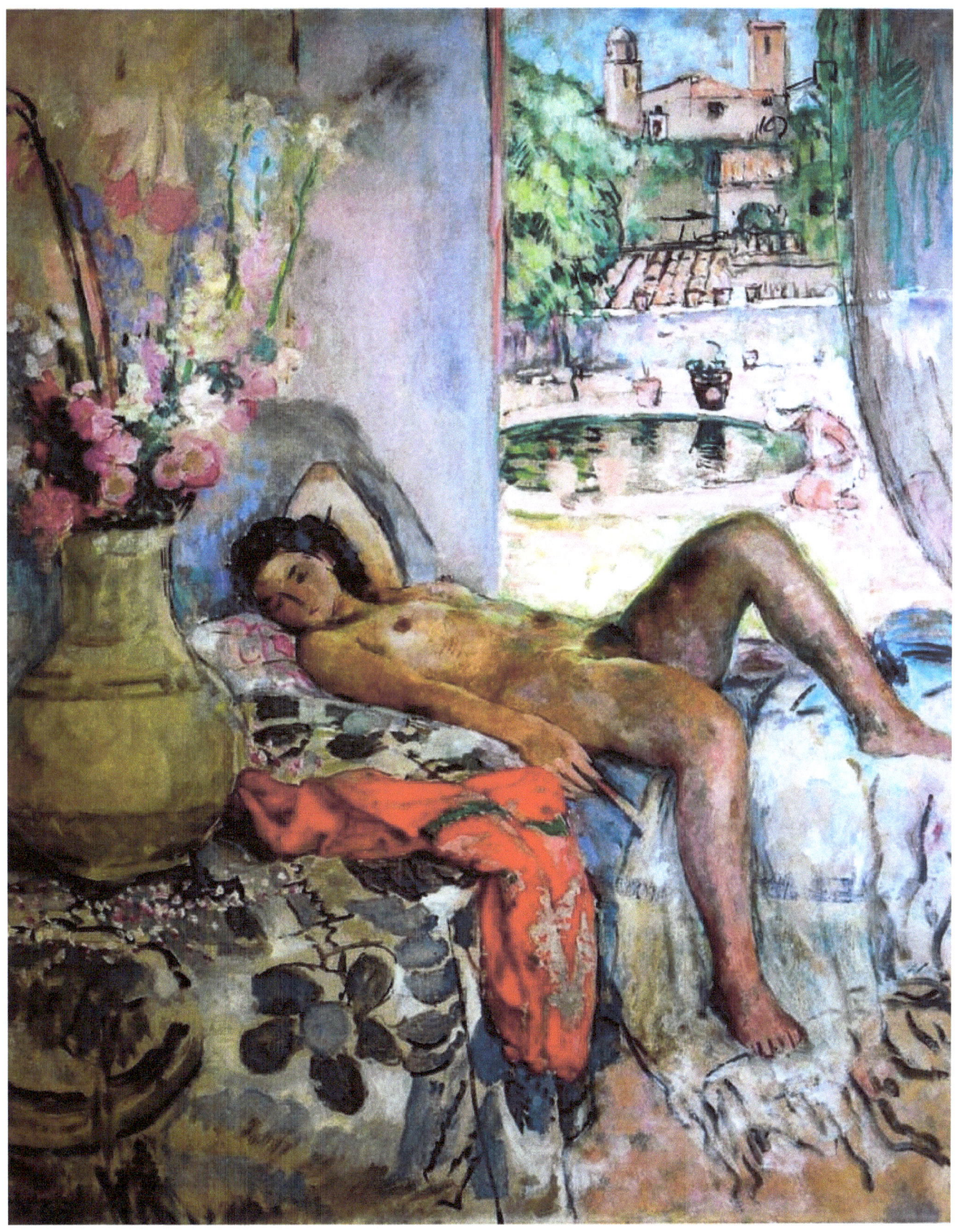

Girl with Blue Veil by Gustav Klimt

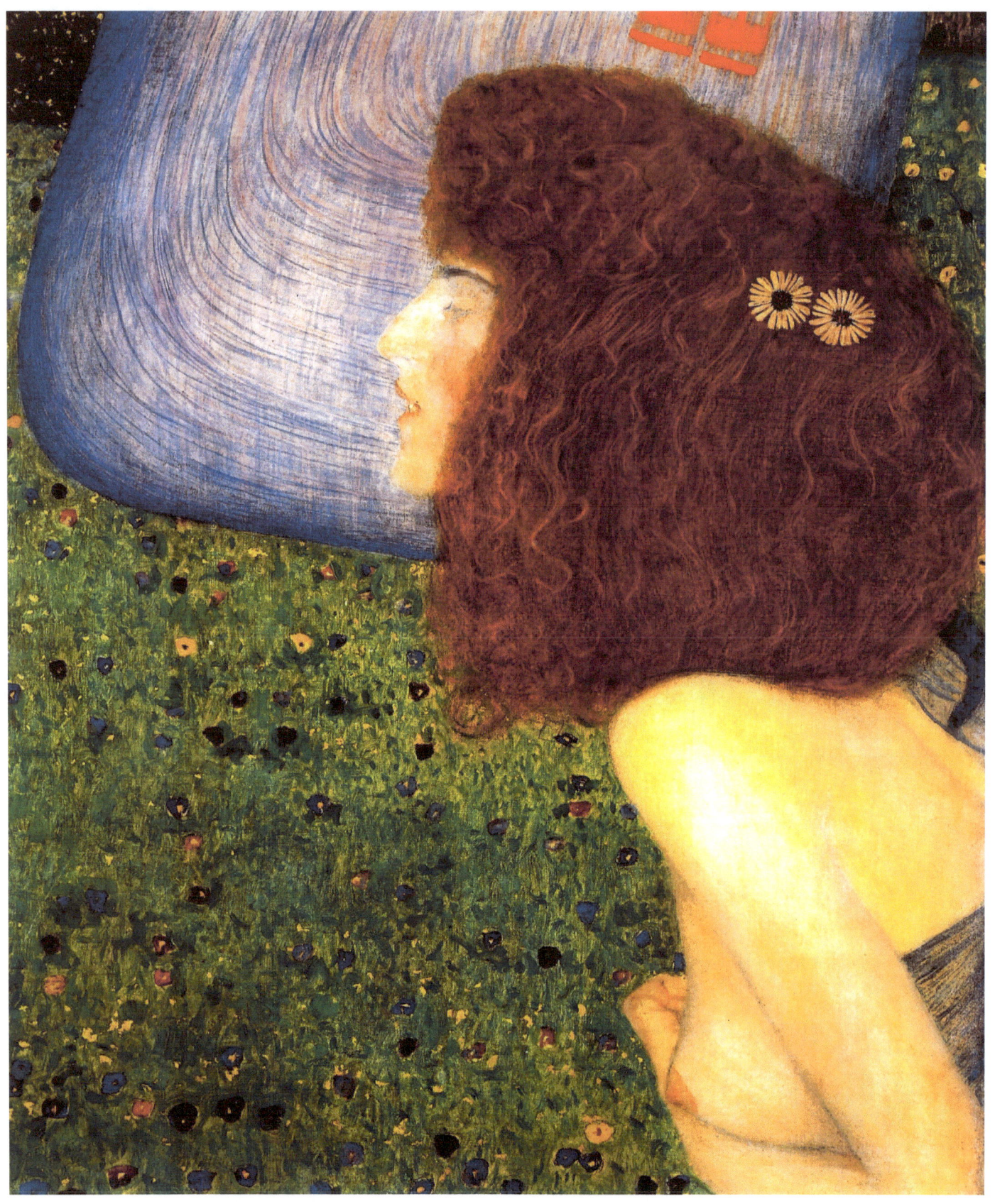

Ancient Chinese Erotica – Nude Couple by Unknown

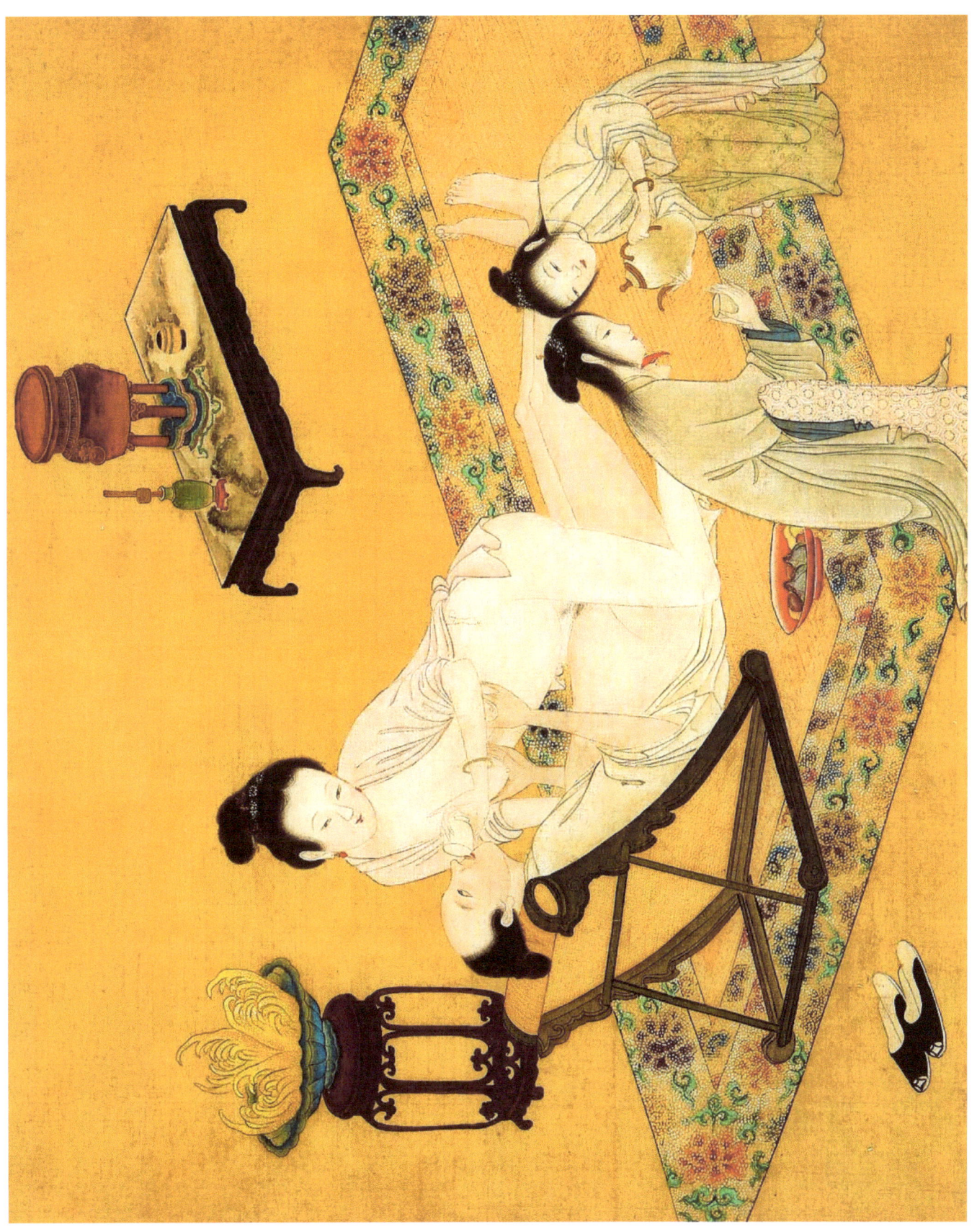

Nude Woman with Black Cat by Alberto Vargas

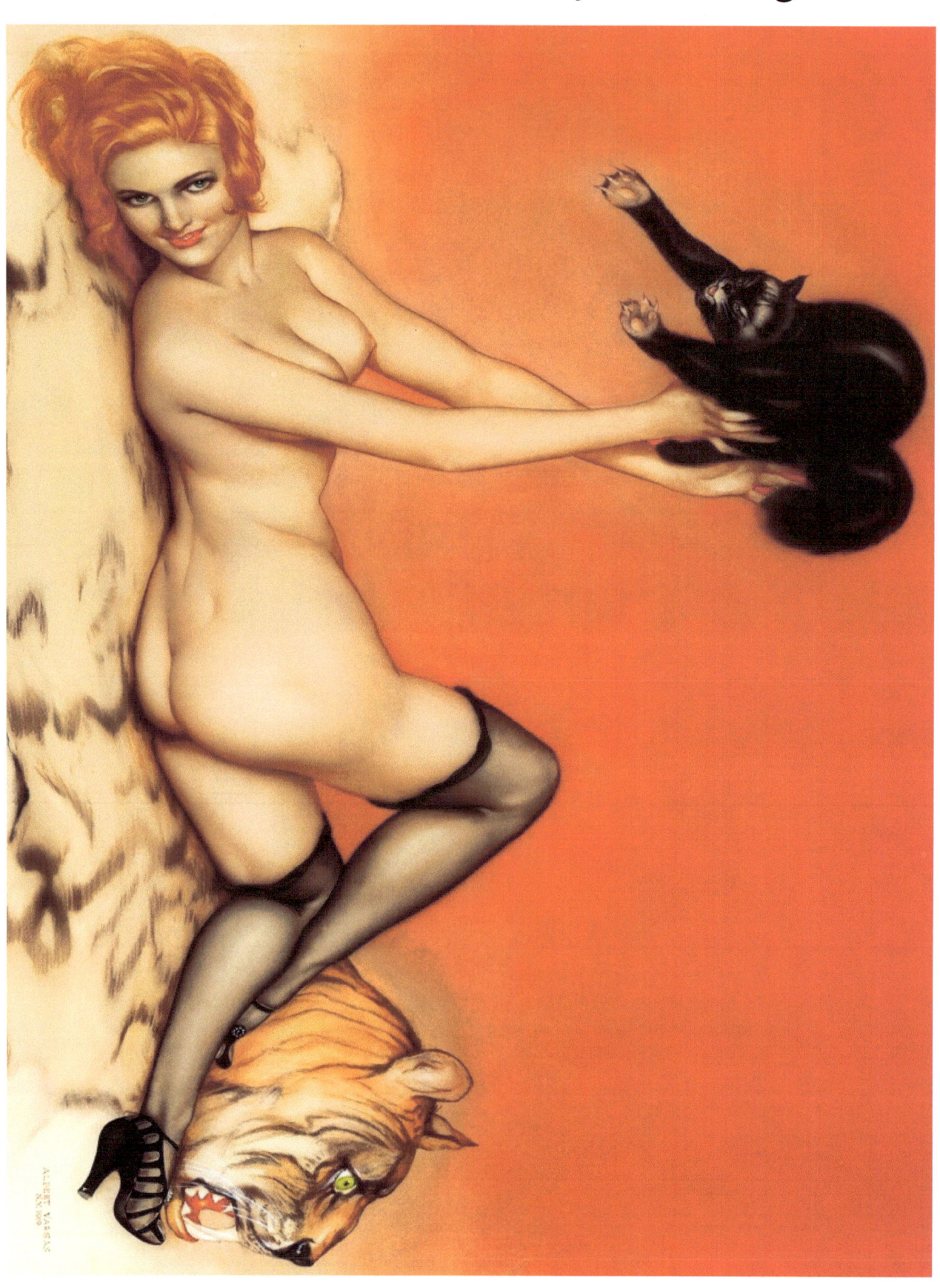

Lassitude - Nude Woman with Eyes Closed by Gari Melchers

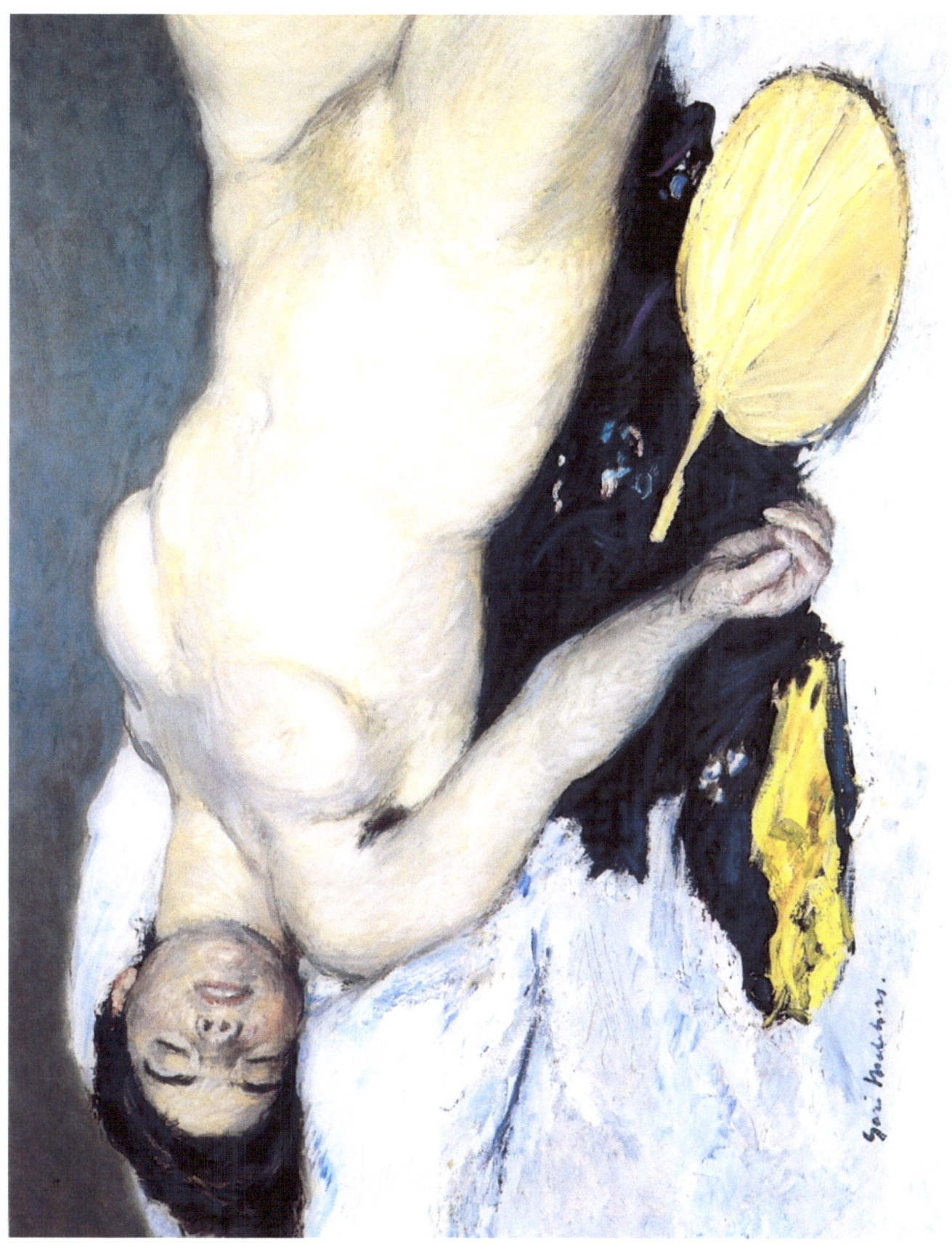

Nude 1914 by Murayama Kaita

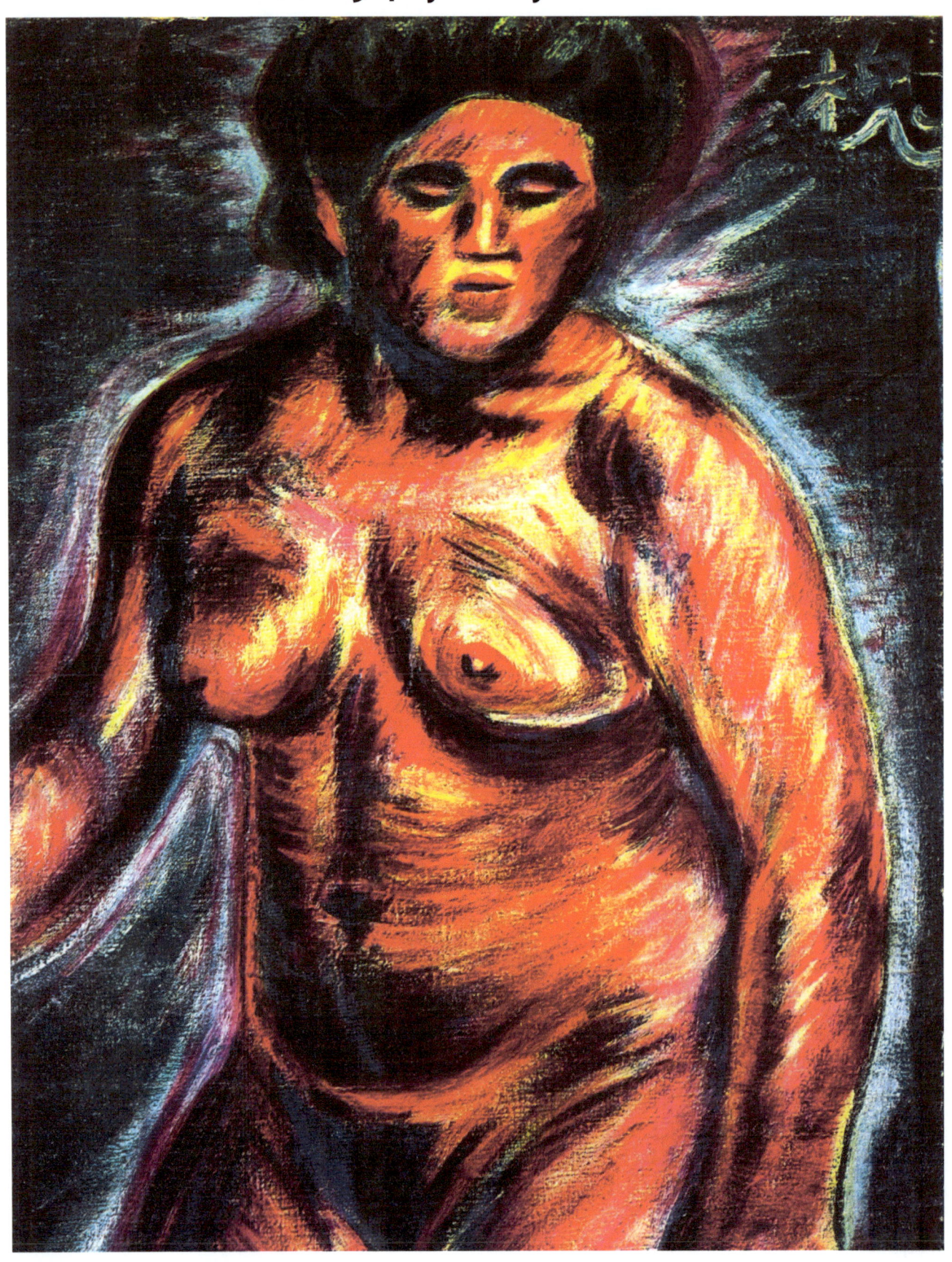

About The Author

The author of this work currently resides in a small coastal town in Southern Oregon. He owns a small photography publishing business and continues to work on new pictorial books as well as writing poetry, stories and some non-fiction works.

Other Books by the Author on Amazon

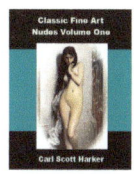
"Classic Fine Art Nudes: Volume One." - This book features a collection of classic fine art nudes and is available on Amazon at https://www.amazon.com/Classic-Fine-Art-Nudes-One/dp/1093912073.

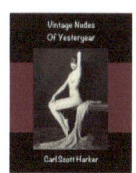
"Vintage Nudes of Yesteryear" presents sixty-five black and white photos of nude women produced generally between the years 1900 and 1923. It can be found on Amazon here: https://www.amazon.com/Vintage-Nudes-Yesteryear-Scott-Harker/dp/107044023X.

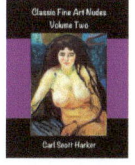
"Classic Fine Art Nudes: Volume Two." - This book is the second book in a series collecting classic fine art nudes and is available on Amazon at https://www.amazon.com/Classic-Fine-Art-Nudes-Two/dp/1711917583.

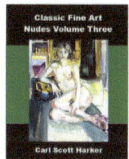
"Classic Fine Art Nudes: Volume Three." This book is the third book in a series collecting classic fine art nudes and is available on Amazon at https://amzn.to/3mAAK1N.

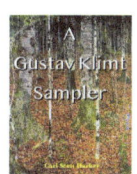
"A Gustav Klimt Sampler" – Here is a collection of 46 paintings and drawings by the Austrian artist Gustav Klimt. This is a sampling of his best work. The book is available on Amazon at https://www.amazon.com/Gustav-Klimt-Sampler-Great-Artists-ebook/dp/B084V1W3L7.

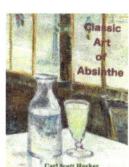
"Classic Art of Absinthe" - This book collects the best of the classic artwork about absinthe from the makers of absinthe, those who wanted absinthe banned and the artists of the time (mid-1800's to early 1900's). It is available on Amazon at https://www.amazon.com/Classic-Absinthe-Carl-Scott-Harker/dp/1653501189.

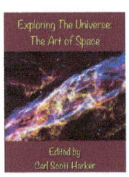 **"Exploring The Universe: The Art of Space"** - Through the use of instruments such as the Hubble Space Telescope, scientists have captured the colorful art that space itself creates. Here is the link: https://www.amazon.com/Exploring-Universe-Carl-Scott-Harker-ebook/dp/B077XQRPQL

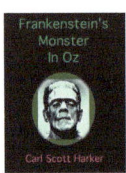 **"Frankenstein's Monster in Oz"** - This book tells the story of how Frankenstein's Monster comes to Oz and what happens to him there. It is available on Amazon at https://www.amazon.com/Frankensteins-Monster-Carl-Scott-Harker/dp/1707291365.

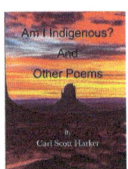 **"Am I Indigenous and Other Poems"** – A collection of poems written between late 2016 and Autumn 2019. This book can be found on Amazon here: https://www.amazon.com/Am-I-Indigenous-Other-Poems/dp/1689862424.

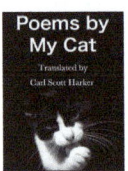 **"Poems By My Cat"** – These poems reveal how cats view the world. The book can be found on Amazon here: https://www.amazon.com/Poems-Cat-Carl-Scott-Harker/dp/1793903239.

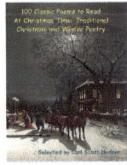 **"100 Classic Poems to Read at Christmas Time"** Here is a collection of some of the best Christmas poems written. The book can be found here: https://www.amazon.com/dp/B07J9YS7QK

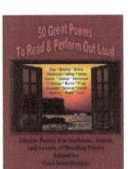 **"50 Great Poems to Read & Perform Out Loud"** - This is a collection of the best poems ever written. The book can be found here: https://amzn.to/2zz8GFT.

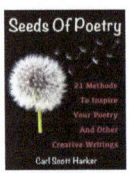 **"Seeds of Poetry: 21 Methods to Inspire Your Poetry and Other Creative Writings"** – a book featuring writing tips with examples to inspire the writing of your own poetry and other creative works. You will find this book here: https://amzn.to/2HtMpO7.

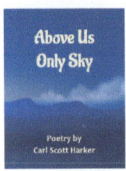 **"Above Us Only Sky"** – This book of poetry features poems written between late April, 2020 to late October, 2020. You will find this book here: https://amzn.to/38kb83R.

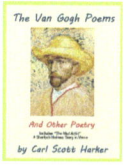 **"The Van Gogh Poems and Other Poetry"** - This book features a collection of poems written in late 2019 and early 2020. The first seventeen poem were inspired by paintings by Vincent Van Gogh. The book is available on Amazon at https://amzn.to/38Hq6Tg.

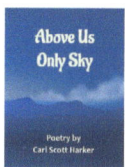 **"Above Us Only Sky"** – This book of poetry features poems written between late April, 2020 to late October, 2020. You will find this book here: https://amzn.to/38kb83R.

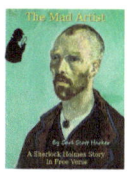 **"The Mad Artist: A Sherlock Holmes Story in Free Verse"** This book presents a new Sherlock Holmes story and is written in free verse and features the artist Vincent Van Gogh. It is available on Amazon at https://amzn.to/36nWvf0.

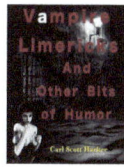 **"Vampire Limericks and Other Bits of Humor"** - This book collects my early work prior to the year 2000 (mostly) and includes limericks, cartoons and a short story. Here is the link to the book on Amazon: https://amzn.to/2IsPUbg.